NEGRO(W)

THE GROWTH WITHIN STARTS WITH YOU.

BY:

AL MADDIN

Table of Contents

· · · · · · · · · ● · · · · · · · · ·

Introduction:
Why "Negrow"?

I wrote this book because I wanted to give people just like me a strategic guide towards breaking mental barriers and expanding their minds. Growing up in certain environments can make you feel stuck, and I know that feeling all too well. Growing up in Detroit, a city renowned for its strength and tenacity, I once felt the weight of limitations pressing down upon me. I saw the struggles, the broken dreams, and the seemingly insurmountable obstacles that surrounded me. But within that challenging environment, I discovered an inner strength—a seed of possibility that, when nurtured, began to sprout and flourish. It was through intentional self-growth and embracing change that I was able to break free from the confines of my circumstances.

Through my own journey of personal growth and transformation, I discovered that there is always hope, even in the most challenging circumstances. I realized that the power to break free from the shackles of our environment lies within each of us. It was in this realization that I became compelled to share my experiences and insights, offering a guiding light for others who may feel trapped and yearn for change.

I wanted to redefine the word "negro" and give it a new meaning. Originally, "negro" was a term associated with the painful history of racial oppression and discrimination. However, I believe it's time to infuse this word with a powerful and positive connotation. From now on, we will use "NEGROW" as a symbol of growth, resilience, and the limitless potential that resides within each of us.

With this book, I invite you to join me on a transformative journey. Together, we will step out of our comfort zones, defy the limitations that have been imposed upon us, and embark on a path of personal growth and fulfillment. Drawing upon my own experiences and the wisdom gained along the way, I will provide you with practical strategies and insights to break free from the mental barriers that have held you back.

This book is a testament to the transformative power of personal growth. It is a testament to the fact that, regardless of where we come from or what challenges we face, we all possess the innate capacity to rise above our circumstances and achieve greatness. I want you to know that it's not too late. It's never too late to embark on a journey of personal growth and transformation.

Through the strategies and insights shared in this book, I aim to guide you towards breaking those mental barriers that have held you back for far too long. Together, we will explore the power of mindset, resilience, self-belief, and embracing change. We will tap into the wellspring of potential within ourselves and rewrite the narrative of our lives.

Moreover, I recognize the influence of our family trees on our lives. The patterns and experiences passed down through generations can shape our perspectives and limit our possibilities. But I firmly believe that we can change the health of our family tree. By breaking the cycle of stagnation, by refusing to accept limitations, and by embracing personal growth, we have the power to transform not only our own lives but also the lives of future generations.

As I share these words with you, I am humbled and grateful. I thank God for entrusting me with His people and for giving me the words to say. It is a divine purpose that drives me to empower others and provide them with the tools they need to embrace growth.

So, join me on this transformative journey. Let's shatter the mental barriers that have held us back, embrace change, and step into a future filled with hope and possibility. Success has no age limit, and your time is now. Together, we can unlock the immense potential within us and create a life that is truly fulfilling. Together, let's cultivate our seeds of greatness and watch them blossom.

Embracing Our Power:
Black Excellence in Style, Creativity, and the Future

······●·●·●·●·●·**●**·●·●·●·●·●······

Introduction:

As black individuals, we often overlook the immense power we possess. From shaping trends in style and creativity to forging the path towards a brighter future, our contributions have been profound. However, we must recognize that we have inadvertently allowed others to appropriate and profit from our cultural innovations. It is time to reclaim our narrative, build our own platforms, and safeguard what is rightfully ours. By doing so, we will not only preserve our heritage but also leave a lasting legacy for generations to come.

Unleashing the Power of Style and Creativity:

Throughout history, black people have been at the forefront of style and fashion, redefining and shaping the very notion of what is considered "cool." From the vibrant expression of African prints to the elegance of black-owned luxury brands, we have consistently set the bar high. Our unique sense of style has influenced mainstream fashion, yet we often do not receive the credit or financial gain we deserve. By recognizing our power, we can create avenues to support and promote black-owned fashion businesses and designers, ensuring that our creativity remains firmly in our hands.

Harnessing Creativity to Shape the Future:

Creativity is the driving force behind progress, and black individuals have long been at the vanguard of groundbreaking artistic and cultural movements. From music genres like jazz, blues, and hip-hop to influential literary works and visual arts, we have shaped and revolutionized various creative landscapes. It is crucial that we continue to nurture and celebrate our artistic endeavors, establishing platforms that amplify our voices and talents. By doing so, we not only inspire future generations but also shape a future that embraces and values our contributions.

Taking Back the Canvas:

For far too long, we have built the canvas of culture and creativity, only to watch others come in and add their strokes without due recognition or compensation. It is time to reclaim our rightful place at the center of these narratives, ensuring that our stories are told and our voices are heard. This requires actively supporting and uplifting black artists, creators, and entrepreneurs, promoting their work and endeavors through various channels. By building and maintaining our own platforms, we can foster an environment where black excellence thrives and our contributions are celebrated and respected.

Preserving for the Future:

As we strive to reclaim our power, it is essential to look beyond the present and think about the future. By actively building and preserving our own institutions, businesses, and communities, we lay the foundation for future generations to inherit and build upon. This involves passing down our knowledge, fostering mentorship programs, and providing opportunities for young black individuals to flourish in various creative fields. By doing so, we ensure that the power we reclaim today becomes an enduring legacy for the generations yet to come.

Conclusion:

As black individuals, we hold within us a remarkable power to shape the world through style, creativity, and innovation. It is time to recognize and embrace this power, reclaiming the narratives and industries that have been co-opted from us. By building our own platforms, supporting black-owned businesses and creators, and preserving our cultural heritage, we establish a strong foundation for a future where black excellence is celebrated and continues to thrive. Together, we can forge a path towards a brighter, more equitable future for all.

Invest in Yourself:
The Lifetime Investment:

I n a world filled with endless distractions and fleeting pleasures, it's important to recognize the true value of investing in yourself. While purchasing designer clothes, traveling, or dining at expensive restaurants may provide temporary satisfaction, these material items cannot compare to the lasting benefits that investing in oneself can bring. Investing in yourself is a powerful and transformative act that yields lifelong rewards, empowering you to unlock your full potential and lead a fulfilling life.

When we think of investing, we often associate it with financial ventures or acquiring assets. However, the most valuable investment you can make is in yourself. This type of investment goes beyond material possessions and delves into personal growth, skill development, and self-improvement. It is an investment that pays dividends for a lifetime.

Investing in yourself requires a commitment of time, effort, and resources. Just like buying designer clothes or indulging in lavish experiences, it comes with a cost. However, the difference lies in the returns you receive. Material possessions offer temporary satisfaction, but investing in yourself leads to personal growth, increased knowledge, improved skills, and enhanced well-being.

One of the most significant advantages of investing in yourself is the lifelong impact it can have. While material possessions may lose their novelty over time, the knowledge, skills, and experiences gained through personal investment stay with you forever. By acquiring new skills, pursuing higher education, or honing your talents, you not only broaden your horizons but also create a foundation for ongoing success and personal fulfillment.

Investing in yourself also strengthens your self-confidence and resilience. As you challenge yourself and push beyond your comfort zone, you develop a sense of self-assurance that extends far beyond any material possession. This newfound confidence allows you to tackle obstacles with determination, take calculated risks, and embrace new opportunities that arise along your journey.

Moreover, investing in yourself nurtures personal well-being and happiness. Engaging in activities that promote self-care, such as exercising regularly, practicing mindfulness, or pursuing hobbies you love, nourishes your mind, body, and soul. By prioritizing your well-being, you build a solid foundation for overall happiness and contentment.

Investing in yourself is a lifelong commitment that manifests in various forms. It can involve enrolling in educational courses or workshops, seeking mentorship, attending seminars or conferences, reading books, or even embarking on a journey of self-discovery. The choices are endless, and the investment can be tailored to suit your unique aspirations, interests, and goals.

Ultimately, investing in yourself is an act of self-love and self-worth. It demonstrates that you value your growth and development, and believe in your potential to create a fulfilling and successful life. By prioritizing personal investment, you open the doors to a world of possibilities, continuous growth, and lifelong satisfaction.

So, the next time you find yourself contemplating a purchase of temporary pleasure, consider redirecting those resources towards investing in yourself. Instead of acquiring yet another material possession, seek opportunities for personal growth, knowledge acquisition, skill development, and self-improvement. The returns you receive will far surpass the temporary satisfaction of material possessions, as you embark on a lifelong journey of self-discovery, success, and lasting fulfillment. Invest in yourself, and reap the rewards that will last a lifetime.

Investing in Our Future:
Moving Beyond Material Competition

Introduction:

In today's fast-paced consumerist culture, there is an underlying tendency to constantly purchase items as a means of competing with others or trying to outdo one another. This "one-upmanship" mentality has become deeply ingrained in our society, with individuals striving to display their wealth and status through material possessions. However, it is important to reflect on the long-term impact of our actions and consider redirecting our resources towards investments that can benefit future generations, namely our children. By shifting our focus from instant gratification to creating a legacy for our offspring, we can pave the way for a more sustainable and prosperous future.

The Allure of Material Competition:

The desire to keep up with the Joneses and maintain a certain level of social status has been a driving force behind the rampant consumerism prevalent in our culture. Whether it's the latest gadgets, luxurious cars, designer clothes, or extravagant vacations, we often find ourselves caught up in a cycle of relentless spending. We are led to believe that owning more or having something better than our peers will bring us happiness and fulfillment. However, this pursuit of material possessions can be fleeting, leaving us constantly yearning for the next big purchase, perpetuating a cycle of discontentment.

Redefining Success:

Rather than measuring success solely by the accumulation of material wealth, it is crucial to shift our perspective towards investing in a better future for our children. This redefinition of success involves focusing on long-term planning and considering the impact of our actions on future generations. It is about breaking free from the cycle of immediate gratification and embracing a mindset that values sustainability, growth, and the legacy we leave behind.

Investing in the Future:

One of the most powerful ways to create a lasting impact for our children is by redirecting our financial resources towards investments that can secure their future. Instead of spending excessive amounts on temporary luxuries, we can explore avenues such as education funds, real estate, stocks, or starting a business that can provide long-term benefits. By investing wisely, we not only build a solid foundation for our children's financial well-being but also teach them valuable lessons about financial responsibility and the importance of planning for the future.

Embracing Sustainability:

Investing in our children's future goes beyond financial matters. It also entails nurturing values, knowledge, and skills that will equip them to thrive in a rapidly changing world. By focusing on education, personal growth, and character development, we empower our children to become resilient, adaptable individuals who can overcome challenges and contribute positively to society. By investing in their intellectual and emotional development, we lay the groundwork for a future generation that is equipped to make a difference.

Conclusion:

Our culture's obsession with material competition and instant gratification often distracts us from the more meaningful aspects of life. However, by reevaluating our priorities and redirecting our resources towards investments that benefit our children's future, we can break free from this cycle and create a legacy that extends beyond our own lifetimes. It is crucial to embrace a mindset that values sustainability, growth, and leaving a positive impact for the next generation. By investing in our children's financial, intellectual, and emotional well-being, we can ensure that they inherit a world that is better equipped for their success and fulfillment.

Setting Examples for Our Children:
Creating a Brighter Path Forward

······ ● ● ● ● ● ● ● ● ● ● ● ● ● ● ······

Introduction:

In the journey of parenthood, it is crucial to recognize that our children's potential is intrinsically tied to our own. As parents, we bear the responsibility of not only nurturing and supporting our children but also setting examples that inspire and empower them to reach greater heights. By establishing positive role models and fostering a mindset of continuous growth and learning, we can pave the way for our children's success and shield them from the struggles we ourselves have endured. This realization underscores the importance of personal development, education, and the passing down of knowledge to ensure a brighter future for our offspring.

Leading by Example:

Children learn through observation, and as parents, our actions have a profound impact on their development. If we want our children to dream big, embrace challenges, and achieve their goals, we must demonstrate these qualities ourselves. Setting examples means embodying the values we wish to instill in our children, such as perseverance, integrity, empathy, and a thirst for knowledge.

When children witness their parents actively pursuing personal growth, whether through further education, professional development, or cultivating new skills, they understand the importance of continuous learning. By showing a genuine interest in expanding our knowledge and broadening our horizons, we teach our children the value of intellectual curiosity and the limitless possibilities that come with it.

Creating a New Path:

To shield our children from the struggles we have faced, we must actively work towards creating a new path for them. This involves overcoming obstacles, breaking cycles, and challenging outdated norms. By analyzing our own experiences and identifying areas for improvement, we can carve out a better future for our children.

Breaking through barriers, whether they are societal, economic, or personal, requires resilience and determination. By confronting our own limitations and striving for personal growth, we inspire our children to do the same. We show them that setbacks are not permanent roadblocks but opportunities for growth and transformation.

Passing Down Knowledge:

Knowledge is a powerful tool that can be inherited across generations. As parents, it is our duty to impart wisdom and share the lessons we have learned along the way. By passing down knowledge, we equip our children with a solid foundation on which they can build their own success stories.

Education is not limited to formal schooling but encompasses a broad range of experiences. Engaging in meaningful conversations, sharing personal anecdotes, and encouraging critical thinking are all ways in which we can actively contribute to our children's intellectual development. By nurturing a love for learning, we instill in them the confidence to explore new ideas, adapt to change, and make informed decisions.

Conclusion:

Our children's future is intimately intertwined with our own actions and choices. By recognizing that they are likely to follow in our footsteps, we bear the responsibility to set positive examples and create a new path forward for them. We must invest in our own personal growth, challenge the status quo, and pass down knowledge to empower our children to surpass the struggles we have faced. In doing so, we can inspire a generation that thrives, learns, and achieves beyond our wildest dreams.

The Inheritance of Knowledge:
Beyond Monetary Wealth

·········•••• ● •••··········

Introduction:

In a world often fixated on financial inheritance, it is essential to recognize that money is not the sole legacy we leave behind. While wealth can provide comfort and security, there exists a wealth of intangible and invaluable assets that can be passed down from one generation to another. Among these precious inheritances is knowledge—the timeless wisdom, experiences, and insights that shape individuals, families, and societies. In this article, we explore the profound impact of passing down knowledge and highlight its significance alongside monetary inheritance.

The Power of Knowledge:

Knowledge is a transformative force that transcends time and space. Unlike material possessions, it cannot be lost, stolen, or diminished. Instead, it grows and evolves as it is shared and passed on. Whether it is acquired through formal education, life experiences, or personal endeavors, knowledge is a treasure that enriches the lives of those who possess it.

Preserving Traditions and Cultural Heritage:

One of the most remarkable aspects of knowledge inheritance is its ability to preserve traditions and cultural heritage. Through the transfer of knowledge from one generation to the next, customs, values, stories, and rituals are safeguarded, ensuring that the collective identity and wisdom of a community remain intact. This process allows individuals to feel connected to their roots and understand their place in the larger tapestry of history.

Mentorship and Personal Growth:

Knowledge passed down from mentors and elders fosters personal growth and development. Mentors possess a wealth of experience and insights that can guide and inspire younger generations. They provide valuable advice, share lessons learned, and offer perspectives that broaden the horizons of those in their care. Mentorship relationships nurture the next generation's potential, empowering them to overcome challenges and achieve their goals.

Empowering Future Generations:

Transmitting knowledge empowers future generations by equipping them with the tools needed to navigate an ever-changing world. By sharing their expertise, parents, grandparents, and community leaders help younger individuals develop critical thinking skills, problem-solving abilities, and emotional intelligence. This inheritance of knowledge enables individuals to make informed decisions, contribute to their communities, and shape a better future for themselves and others.

Promoting Innovation and Progress:

Knowledge inheritance serves as a catalyst for innovation and progress. The insights and discoveries of previous generations form the foundation upon which new ideas are built. By passing down knowledge, we provide the building blocks for innovation, inspiring future generations to explore new frontiers, challenge established norms, and make groundbreaking advancements in various fields.

Preserving Intellectual and Artistic Legacies:

Artistic and intellectual creations, too, can be passed down as part of our cultural heritage. Works of literature, music, art, and scientific breakthroughs are not only objects to be admired but also a rich source of knowledge and inspiration. By preserving and sharing these legacies, we ensure that the wisdom, creativity, and contributions of previous generations continue to shape and enrich the world.

Conclusion:

While money certainly holds its value, it is important to recognize that wealth alone does not define a meaningful legacy. The inheritance of knowledge represents an immeasurable gift, capable of inspiring, empowering, and shaping future generations. By passing down knowledge, we bridge the gaps between generations, preserve our cultural heritage, and foster personal and societal growth. So, let us cherish and embrace the power of knowledge as a lasting inheritance, one that can positively impact the world long after we are gone.

The Significance of Traveling:
Expanding Horizons Beyond Our Comfort Zones

·····●●●●●●● ● ●●●●●●·····

Introduction:

In today's fast-paced world, we often find ourselves caught up in our daily routines and surrounded by the familiar comforts of our local environment. While indulging in fancy restaurants and impulsive purchases can bring temporary satisfaction, there is an alternative that offers far more profound benefits: traveling. By allocating resources and saving up for a journey, we can break free from the confines of our routine and embark on an adventure that broadens our perspective and reveals the boundless possibilities that life has to offer.

1. Stepping Out of Our Comfort Zones:

Traveling necessitates stepping out of our comfort zones and immersing ourselves in unfamiliar surroundings. When we venture beyond the familiar, we are confronted with new cultures, languages, and perspectives. This exposure stimulates personal growth, fostering adaptability, open-mindedness, and empathy. It allows us to challenge preconceived notions and expand our understanding of the world.

2. Discovering New Horizons:

By exploring different regions and countries, we are exposed to diverse landscapes, histories, and traditions. We can witness breath-taking natural wonders, explore architectural marvels, and engage with cultural heritage. Each destination offers a unique tapestry of experiences, from interacting with locals and trying new cuisines to partaking in traditional festivities. These encounters enrich our lives and broaden our horizons, showing us that life's possibilities extend far beyond our place of origin.

3. Fostering Personal Transformation:

Traveling offers a profound opportunity for personal transformation. As we detach ourselves from our daily routines, we gain a fresh perspective on our lives, values, and priorities. Being immersed in new environments and engaging with different people challenges our assumptions and helps us reevaluate our own belief systems. This introspection can lead to self-discovery, increased self-confidence, and a clearer sense of purpose.

4. Fueling Creativity and Imagination:

Exploring new landscapes, architecture, art, and cultures can ignite our creativity and inspire us in unexpected ways. Traveling exposes us to a plethora of artistic expressions and sparks our imagination. The vibrant colors, intricate designs, and captivating stories we encounter can stimulate new ideas and perspectives. By breaking away from our routine, we allow ourselves to see the world through fresh eyes and unlock our creative potential.

5. Embracing the Endless Possibilities:

As we embark on journeys and witness the richness of the world, we realize that the possibilities for personal growth and exploration are truly endless. Our experiences while traveling serve as a reminder that life is not confined to a singular place or stage. By venturing beyond our comfort zones, we create a mindset of continuous growth and curiosity, inspiring us to seek out new adventures and embrace opportunities that come our way.

Conclusion:

Traveling is not merely about indulging in fancy restaurants or impulsive purchases; it is about investing in experiences that expand our horizons and transform our lives. Stepping outside our comfort zones and exploring new environments enables personal growth, fosters creativity, and reveals the vast possibilities that exist beyond our current stage in life. So, let us save up a little extra, pack our bags, and embark on a journey of self-discovery and endless exploration. By doing so, we open ourselves up to a world brimming with opportunities and embrace the true richness of life.

Taking Responsibility:
Moving Beyond Blaming Our Parents

Introduction:

It is a common tendency for individuals to attribute their shortcomings and limitations to their parents. However, it is essential to recognize that our parents can only guide us as far as they themselves have progressed. They can teach us only what they know and have experienced. Rather than blaming them for our perceived inadequacies, it is crucial to acknowledge their limitations and take responsibility for our own growth and development. This article explores the importance of understanding the role of our parents in our lives and emphasizes the need to move forward by filling in the gaps in our knowledge and experiences.

Understanding Our Parents' Limitations:

Our parents are human beings with their own unique backgrounds, experiences, and knowledge. They have their own sets of strengths and weaknesses. They have likely done their best to provide us with love, care, and guidance based on their understanding and capabilities. It is important to acknowledge that they, too, were shaped by their own upbringing and life experiences, which may have influenced their ability to equip us with certain skills or knowledge.

Learning from Their Journey:

While our parents may not have been able to provide us with everything we need, their journey can still serve as a valuable source of learning. We can learn from their triumphs and mistakes, their values and beliefs, and the wisdom they have accumulated over the years. By observing their lives, we can gain insight into what worked for them and what did not, allowing us to make informed choices as we navigate our own paths.

Taking Responsibility for Our Growth:

Blaming our parents for our shortcomings is an easy way to avoid taking responsibility for our own lives. However, true growth comes from acknowledging that we are responsible for our own actions, decisions, and personal development. It is crucial to understand that we have the power to shape our own destinies, regardless of the circumstances in which we were raised.

Filling in the Gaps:

Recognizing that our parents' guidance has limitations means understanding that we may have missed out on certain experiences or knowledge. However, this realization also presents an opportunity for personal growth. We have the ability to seek out new experiences, learn from others, and broaden our horizons beyond what our parents were able to offer. By proactively seeking knowledge, pursuing our passions, and surrounding ourselves with diverse perspectives, we can fill in the gaps in our education and experiences.

Seeking Mentors and Role Models:

In addition to our parents, there are numerous individuals who can serve as mentors and role models in our lives. These individuals, whether they are teachers, friends, or professionals in our chosen fields, can provide us with guidance and support as we strive to develop new skills and knowledge. By seeking out these mentors and role models, we can expand our horizons and learn from their expertise, helping us to bridge the gap between what our parents could provide and what we need to thrive.

Conclusion:

Blaming our parents for our perceived shortcomings only hinders our personal growth and development. Instead, we must recognize their limitations and take responsibility for our own lives. We should strive to learn from their experiences while acknowledging that we have the power to shape our own destinies. By actively seeking new knowledge and experiences, and by seeking out mentors and role models, we can fill in the gaps left by our parents and create a path of success and fulfillment that is uniquely our own.

Healing is Important:
Addressing Childhood Traumas and Emotional Wounds

·········•·•·•·•·•·⬤·•·•·•·•·•·•·········

In the journey of life, each of us carries a unique tapestry of experiences and emotions. Among these, some wounds run deep, originating from our childhood traumas. Unfortunately, many of us go through life carrying these burdens without even realizing it. As time goes on, we become accustomed to the weight, often numbing ourselves to the fact that we are still in need of healing. Consequently, we unintentionally transfer our pain onto others, unintentionally bleeding onto those who did not inflict the wounds upon us. It is essential, therefore, to recognize the significance of healing and take proactive steps to address the residual traumas that persist within us.

Childhood traumas have a profound impact on our lives, shaping our beliefs, behaviors, and emotional well-being. They can stem from various sources such as neglect, abuse, violence, or witnessing distressing events. These experiences imprint themselves onto our minds and hearts, leaving lasting imprints that impact our relationships, self-worth, and overall quality of life.

One of the unfortunate aspects of trauma is its ability to conceal itself. We may grow accustomed to our emotional pain, adapting to its presence until it becomes a normalized part of our existence. This normalization can lead us to believe that we have moved on, that we have healed, while deep-seated wounds continue to affect us subconsciously. Unresolved childhood traumas have a way of resurfacing, manifesting as triggers in certain situations or patterns of behavior that we may not understand.

The consequences of unhealed wounds are far-reaching, particularly when it comes to our relationships. We might find ourselves reacting disproportionately to situations or overreacting to seemingly insignificant triggers. Our past hurts can unconsciously dictate our actions, leading to patterns of self-sabotage or damaging interactions with others. By projecting our pain onto unsuspecting individuals, we inadvertently perpetuate a cycle of hurt and retraumatization.

Recognizing the need for healing is the first step towards breaking this cycle. It requires us to acknowledge that we are not as whole as we might think, that the pain from our past experiences still lingers within us. By opening ourselves up to this realization, we allow ourselves the opportunity to embark on a journey of self-discovery and transformation.

Healing is a multifaceted process that varies for each individual. It involves delving into the depths of our emotional wounds, facing the pain head-on, and seeking appropriate support and guidance. Therapy, counseling, and support groups can provide a safe space for us to explore our past, gain insight, and learn coping mechanisms. These resources offer valuable tools to navigate the complex terrain of healing, providing a sense of validation, understanding, and empowerment.

Additionally, self-care practices play a crucial role in the healing process. Engaging in activities that bring joy, practicing mindfulness, nurturing our physical and emotional well-being, and setting healthy boundaries can all contribute to our overall healing. It's essential to cultivate self-compassion, understanding that healing takes time and patience.

As we embark on our healing journey, we must be mindful of the potential impact our unhealed wounds have on others. Taking responsibility for our actions and seeking to break the cycle of pain is a vital aspect of our growth. By acknowledging our own wounds and actively working towards healing, we can prevent ourselves from bleeding onto those who do not deserve our pain.

In conclusion, healing is of utmost importance, especially when it comes to addressing childhood traumas and emotional wounds. Recognizing that we carry unresolved pain allows us to break free from the cycle of retraumatization. By actively seeking healing, we can transform ourselves, our relationships, and ultimately create a more compassionate and empathetic world. Through self-awareness, self-care, and seeking appropriate support, we can mend our wounds, restore our well-being, and foster healthier connections with ourselves and others.

Wake up.. Pray... Meditate.... Focus...

S tarting the day with intention and mindfulness is a powerful way to set yourself up for a great day. As the world slowly awakens around you, taking a few moments to gather your thoughts and connect with your inner self can have a profound impact on your overall well-being. Whether you follow a specific religious practice or simply engage in a moment of reflection, the act of praying can provide a sense of grounding and gratitude.

Following prayer, meditation offers an opportunity to cultivate inner peace and clarity. It allows you to let go of any lingering thoughts or worries from the previous day and begin with a clean slate. Through mindful breathing and focusing your attention on the present moment, you can create a calm and centered state of mind. Meditation can also enhance self-awareness, increase focus, and reduce stress levels, enabling you to navigate the day with greater ease.

Focus on having a great day... Focus on the positive things going on in your life...

Consciously directing your focus towards positivity and a great day can significantly influence your overall outlook and experiences. The power of positive thinking is well-documented, and it can shape your attitude and actions throughout the day. By intentionally choosing to focus on the positive aspects of your life, such as gratitude for the relationships you have, the opportunities you enjoy, or the small joys you encounter, you invite more positivity into your day.

Stretch... Work out... Get your blood flowing...

Engaging in physical activity in the morning is an excellent way to invigorate your body and mind. Stretching helps loosen up your muscles and increase flexibility, while working out elevates your heart rate and releases endorphins, creating a natural boost of energy and mood enhancement. Whether it's a brisk walk, a yoga session, or a full workout routine, dedicating time to move your body can promote physical well-being and mental clarity, setting the stage for a productive and energized day ahead.

Create a "To Do" list for the day....

A "To Do" list acts as a guide and roadmap for your day. By organizing your tasks and responsibilities, you gain a clear sense of direction and purpose. Creating a list allows you to prioritize your activities and allocate your time and energy effectively. Breaking down larger tasks into smaller, manageable steps can also help alleviate any feelings of overwhelm and enable you to make progress throughout the day. Crossing items off your list provides a sense of accomplishment and motivation, propelling you forward and increasing your productivity.

In conclusion, the steps outlined above offer a practical and holistic approach to setting yourself up for a great day. By incorporating prayer, meditation, positive focus, physical activity, and effective planning, you create a strong foundation for a fulfilling and productive day. Experiment with these practices, adjust them to fit your unique preferences and lifestyle, and observe how they positively impact your overall well-being and daily experiences. Remember, a great day begins with intentional choices and a positive mindset. So, wake up, try these steps, and embrace the potential of each new day.

4 Things To Always Walk Away From:

In life, we often come across situations and people that can have a negative impact on our well-being. It is important to recognize when it is necessary to distance ourselves from such circumstances and individuals. Here are four things that we should always walk away from in order to maintain a healthy and positive life:

1) Walk away from conversations that involve hate and gossip.

Engaging in conversations filled with hate and gossip can be toxic and detrimental to our own mental and emotional well-being. Participating in such discussions not only promotes negativity but also creates an environment of hostility and resentment. Walking away from these conversations allows us to maintain our own integrity and prevent ourselves from being caught up in unnecessary conflicts. Instead, let's strive to engage in meaningful and uplifting conversations that promote understanding and compassion.

2) Walk away from unnecessary drama.

Drama, whether it arises in our personal relationships, workplace, or social circles, often brings chaos and stress into our lives. Walking away from unnecessary drama means consciously choosing to disengage from situations that don't contribute positively to our growth or well-being. By doing so, we free ourselves from the energy-draining cycle of conflicts, misunderstandings, and emotional turmoil. It allows us to focus our time and energy on more important aspects of our lives that bring us joy and fulfillment.

3) Walk away from people who put you down.

It is crucial to surround ourselves with individuals who uplift, support, and inspire us. Unfortunately, there may be people who constantly put us down, undermine our abilities, or belittle our accomplishments. These toxic relationships can be draining and can erode our self-esteem and self-worth over time. Walking away from such people is an act of self-care and self-respect. It allows us to create space for positive relationships and build a supportive network that encourages personal growth and happiness.

4) Walk away from the table if respect is no longer being served.

Respect is the foundation of any healthy and harmonious relationship, be it personal or professional. When respect is compromised, it becomes essential to reassess the dynamics of that relationship. If we find ourselves constantly disrespected, disregarded, or mistreated, it is crucial to walk away from the table. Staying in a situation where respect is lacking only perpetuates a cycle of negativity and can have a detrimental effect on our self-worth and overall well-being. Walking away in such circumstances allows us to reclaim our dignity and seek out relationships that value and honor our presence.

In conclusion, walking away from certain situations and people is not a sign of weakness, but rather an act of strength and self-preservation. By choosing to walk away from conversations filled with hate and gossip, unnecessary drama, people who put us down, and situations where respect is absent, we create a space for positivity, personal growth, and genuine connections. It is essential to prioritize our own well-being and surround ourselves with individuals and experiences that contribute to our happiness and success.

Uplift Yourself Today:
Embrace Your Potential and Achieve Greatness

············ ● ● ●············

Introduction:

In a world where self-doubt and negativity can easily consume our thoughts, it is essential to consciously uplift ourselves, motivate, and inspire our own selves. By acknowledging our abilities, progress, and embracing positive thoughts, we can tap into our unlimited potential and achieve extraordinary things. This page serves as a reminder and guide to empower you on your journey of self-motivation and self-belief. So, take a moment, inhale positivity, and let's embark on a transformative path together.

Believe in Your Abilities:

First and foremost, remind yourself how smart and capable you truly are. We all possess unique talents, skills, and intelligence that contribute to our personal growth and success. Embrace your strengths and nurture them. Reflect on past achievements, both big and small, and recognize the effort, dedication, and determination that propelled you forward. Believe in your abilities, for they are the foundation on which you can build a brighter future.

Reflect on Your Progress:

It's important to pause and acknowledge how far you've come on your journey. Life is a constant evolution, and with each step forward, you accumulate valuable experiences, knowledge, and skills. Take pride in the obstacles you've overcome, the lessons you've learned, and the growth you've achieved. Remind yourself that progress is not always linear, and setbacks are merely stepping stones towards success. Celebrate your resilience and let it fuel your motivation to keep pushing forward.

Bet on Yourself:

In this pursuit of personal and professional goals, it is crucial to bet on yourself. Have faith in your potential and trust that you have what it takes to succeed. Cultivate a mindset of resilience, determination, and a willingness to take calculated risks. Embrace challenges as opportunities for growth and view failures as valuable lessons that bring you closer to your aspirations. By believing in yourself and your dreams, you unlock the power to manifest them into reality.

Fill Yourself with Positive Thoughts:

The mind is a powerful tool that can shape our perception of ourselves and the world around us. Take charge of your thoughts and consciously fill yourself with positivity. Surround yourself with affirmations, inspirational quotes, and motivational resources that uplift your spirit. Replace self-doubt with self-empowering beliefs. Engage in activities that bring you joy and fuel your passion. Remember, a positive mindset is the fuel that propels you toward success.

Chase Your Goals:

No dream is too big or too small. Identify your goals and dreams, no matter how audacious they may seem. Define a clear vision of what you want to achieve, and then commit yourself wholeheartedly to chasing it. Break down your goals into manageable steps and take consistent action towards them. Embrace discipline, perseverance, and a growth mindset. Even on the toughest days, remember that you have the capacity to achieve greatness and turn your dreams into reality.

Conclusion:

Today, and every day, make a conscious effort to uplift, motivate, and inspire yourself. Recognize your intelligence, appreciate your progress, and bet on yourself. Fill your mind with positivity, embrace your goals, and chase them relentlessly. Remember, you possess the power to shape your own destiny and achieve anything you set your mind to. So, go forth with confidence, unleash your potential, and create a life that is truly extraordinary.

Embracing Growth and Redemption:
GOD's Endless Mercy

Introduction:

L ife is a journey filled with ups and downs, triumphs and trib- ulations. Along the way, we inevitably make mistakes, face challenges, and sometimes lose our sense of self. However, in the midst of these struggles, it is crucial to remember that our journey is not over yet. This passage serves as a reminder that regardless of the difficulties we encounter, God's mercy and guidance persist, offering us the opportunity to learn, grow, and find redemption.

Acknowledging Mistakes and Trials:

In the course of our lives, we all make mistakes. We stumble, fall, and occasionally find ourselves on the wrong path. These missteps may lead us to associate with the wrong group of friends, make poor decisions, or lose sight of who we truly are. These experiences can be disheartening and make life feel overwhelming. However, it is essential to recognize that mistakes are a natural part of the human experience. They provide us with valuable lessons and opportunities for personal growth.

Divine Intervention and Unwavering Mercy:

Amidst our darkest moments, it is easy to feel defeated, lost, or abandoned. Nevertheless, this passage offers solace by assuring us that even when life feels unbearable, God's work in our lives is not yet complete. Regardless of our past mistakes or the challenges we currently face, God's unwavering mercy remains a constant force. This unwavering love and guidance give us hope, encouraging us to persevere through the storms and emerge stronger on the other side.

Embracing Growth and Transformation:

The recognition that God is not done with us serves as a powerful motivator to embrace personal growth and transformation. It reminds us that we are not defined by our past errors or present struggles. Instead, we are called to learn from our mistakes, redirect our paths, and seek positive change. Every setback becomes an opportunity to rise, learn, and rebuild our lives with a deeper sense of purpose and understanding.

Faith, Patience, and Trust:

As we navigate the challenges and uncertainties of life, faith, patience, and trust become essential virtues. It is through faith that we believe in the unyielding love and guidance of a higher power. Patience teaches us that personal growth and transformation take time and cannot be rushed. Trusting in God's plan allows us to surrender control and find solace in the knowledge that a greater purpose is at work, even when we cannot see it.

Conclusion:

The passage reminds us that no matter how bleak life may appear at a given moment, God's work in our lives continues. It encourages us to reflect on our past mistakes, recognize our trials as opportunities for growth, and have faith in the endless mercy and love that God extends to us. Embracing personal growth, remaining patient, and trusting in the divine plan will guide us toward redemption, helping us discover our true selves and a fulfilling life. Remember, no matter where we find ourselves, we are not alone, for God's grace and guidance are always available to those who seek them.

Transforming Spending Habits:
From Wants to Wealth Creation

Introduction:

In today's consumer-driven society, it's easy to get caught up in a cycle of spending on countless wants without considering the long-term financial consequences. However, taking a step back to evaluate our expenses and identifying areas where we can redirect our funds towards wealth creation can lead to significant positive changes. In this context, the task at hand urges us to scrutinize our last month's bank statement, identify discretionary expenditures ("wants"), calculate the total, and consider investing half of that amount in ventures that can generate additional income. This exercise aims to highlight the potential for financial growth when we shift our spending habits from instant gratification to long-term wealth creation.

Analyzing the Bank Statement:

The first step in this exercise is to retrieve the bank statement from the previous month. Carefully examining the statement will allow us to gain insight into our spending patterns and distinguish between needs and wants. A need is generally considered an essential expense required for basic survival, such as housing, utilities, groceries, and transportation. Wants, on the other hand, are discretionary purchases that enhance our lifestyle but are not essential for our well-being.

Identifying Wants:

As we go through the bank statement, we need to identify and highlight every expense that falls into the category of wants. This includes expenses related to entertainment, dining out, fashion, hobbies, and luxury items. By highlighting these wants, we gain a clear visual representation of our discretionary spending, often revealing surprising totals that may prompt us to reevaluate our priorities.

Calculating the Total:

Once we have identified and highlighted all the wants on our bank statement, it's time to calculate the total expenditure on these discretionary items. This sum represents the amount of money that could potentially be redirected towards wealth-building activities. Seeing the total can be a startling realization of the substantial funds we allocate to fleeting pleasures and non-essential purchases.

The Shock Factor:

The shock that accompanies realizing the amount spent on wants is a natural response. It underscores the need for a mindset shift from impulsive spending to more intentional financial decisions. While it's essential to enjoy life and indulge in occasional treats, becoming aware of the excessive amounts we allocate to wants can serve as a wake-up call to reevaluate our financial choices.

Investing in Wealth Creation:

Having grasped the impact of our discretionary spending, the next step is to consider allocating at least half of that amount towards investments that have the potential to generate additional income. This could involve exploring various options such as stocks, bonds, real estate, or starting a small business. By redirecting a significant portion of our spending into ventures that can make money, we transition from being mere consumers to becoming proactive participants in our financial future.

Conclusion:

The exercise of analyzing our bank statement and differentiating between wants and needs, followed by reallocating a portion of our discretionary spending into wealth creation endeavors, offers a powerful tool for personal financial growth. By making conscious choices and prioritizing long-term financial goals over immediate gratification, we can begin to build a solid foundation for wealth and financial independence. Remember, transforming spending habits is a gradual process, and small steps taken today can lead to significant outcomes in the future.

Protecting Your Big Dreams:
The Importance of Selective Sharing

· · · · · • • • • ● ● ● • • • • · · ·

Introduction:

In the pursuit of our aspirations and ambitions, we often come across an old adage: "The quickest way to kill a big dream is to introduce it to a small mind." This powerful statement emphasizes the significance of being mindful about whom we choose to share our goals and dreams with. In this essay, we will explore the importance of selective sharing and why it is crucial to protect our dreams from those who may not fully understand or support them.

1. The Power of Perspective:

Sharing our dreams and goals requires vulnerability. When we confide in others, we open ourselves up to their opinions, judgments, and influence. Unfortunately, not everyone possesses the same level of imagination, courage, or belief in what may seem like an audacious endeavor. Small minds, in this context, refer to individuals who lack the ability or inclination to grasp the magnitude or potential of big dreams. Their limited perspective can inadvertently hinder our progress and enthusiasm, ultimately dampening our motivation.

2. Nurturing vs. Negativity:

When we share our dreams with others, we hope for encouragement, support, and constructive feedback. However, small-minded individuals might respond with skepticism, negativity, or discouragement. Their doubts and criticisms can chip away at our self-confidence, leading us to doubt our abilities and question the feasibility of our aspirations. Consequently, it becomes crucial to safeguard our dreams by selectively choosing the people we share them with.

3. The Importance of a Supportive Circle:

Surrounding ourselves with individuals who uplift, inspire, and support us is paramount to achieving our goals. A supportive circle comprises individuals who share our passion, understand our vision, and genuinely believe in our potential. By sharing our dreams with like-minded people, we create an environment that fosters motivation, collaboration, and growth. These individuals can provide valuable insights, offer guidance, and serve as a source of inspiration during challenging times.

4. Shielding Dreams from Negativity:

Not everyone needs to be privy to our dreams and aspirations. It is essential to be discerning when choosing whom to share them with.

Instead of allowing negativity to infiltrate our minds and hinder our progress, we can channel our energy towards seeking out mentors, coaches, or peers who are aligned with our vision. By carefully selecting those with whom we share our dreams, we create a protective shield against discouragement and doubt.

5. Honoring Personal Boundaries:

Selective sharing not only safeguards our dreams but also protects our emotional well-being. Boundaries play a crucial role in ensuring that we do not compromise our dreams or allow them to be diminished by external influences. By defining our limits and being mindful of whom we entrust with our aspirations, we maintain control over our own narrative and preserve the integrity of our dreams.

Conclusion:

In the pursuit of our big dreams, it is essential to be mindful of who we choose to share them with. While it is natural to seek validation and support from others, not everyone may possess the necessary understanding or belief in our aspirations. By selectively sharing our dreams with a supportive circle, we can protect ourselves from negativity, maintain our motivation, and create an environment conducive to growth. Remember, the power to nurture and manifest our dreams ultimately lies within us, and it is our responsibility to guard them wisely.

Perseverance:
The Key to Overcoming Setbacks and Achieving Goals

Introduction:

In our journey towards achieving our goals, setbacks are bound to happen. They can be discouraging, demotivating, and even lead us to question whether we should continue pursuing our aspirations. However, it is essential to understand that giving up on our goals due to one setback is akin to a counterproductive reaction. This analogy, "Giving up on your goal because of one setback is like slashing your other 3 tires because you got one flat," vividly captures the irrationality of abandoning our dreams based on a single setback. By examining this powerful metaphor, we can gain valuable insights into the importance of resilience, determination, and perseverance in the face of adversity.

Exploring the Analogy:

When we encounter a setback, it can feel like a major roadblock preventing us from progressing further. The analogy of slashing three good tires because one tire is flat paints a vivid picture of an illogical response to a temporary setback. Imagine finding yourself with a flat tire while driving. It would be absurd to destroy the remaining three functional tires just because one tire went flat. Doing so would leave us stranded and hinder any chance of reaching our destination. Similarly, giving up on our goals due to a setback deprives us of the opportunity to move forward and accomplish what we set out to do.

The Value of Resilience:

Resilience is a characteristic that separates those who achieve their goals from those who abandon them prematurely. Instead of being disheartened by setbacks, resilient individuals maintain a positive mindset, adapt to challenges, and persist in their pursuit. They view setbacks as temporary obstacles that can be overcome with the right strategies and determination. Just as replacing a flat tire allows us to continue our journey, overcoming setbacks empowers us to keep moving forward towards our goals.

Perseverance as the Driving Force:

Perseverance, often described as the ability to persist in the face of adversity, is essential for achieving long-term success. By sticking to our goals despite setbacks, we build resilience, learn from our experiences, and grow stronger. Each setback becomes an opportunity for personal growth and development. Rather than giving up, we should invest our energy in analyzing what went wrong, identifying areas for improvement, and adjusting our strategies accordingly. Just as we would seek assistance in repairing a flat tire, seeking guidance and support from others can provide fresh perspectives and insights that can help us overcome setbacks and reach our objectives.

Learning from Setbacks:

Setbacks are not indicators of failure but rather lessons that propel us forward. They offer valuable insights into our strengths, weaknesses, and the roadblocks we may encounter on our journey. Each setback presents an opportunity to learn, adapt, and refine our approach. Just as we wouldn't slash our remaining tires if we encountered a flat, we shouldn't let a single setback define our entire journey. Instead, we can use setbacks as stepping stones, learning from them and using the newfound knowledge to make better-informed decisions as we progress.

Conclusion:

The analogy of slashing three good tires due to a flat one serves as a poignant reminder of the irrationality of giving up on our goals because of setbacks. Perseverance, resilience, and a positive mindset are crucial in navigating the challenges we encounter along the way. By embracing setbacks as opportunities for growth and learning, we can continue our pursuit of success. So, let us remember to persevere, keep our eyes on the destination, and stay resilient even in the face of adversity. After all, it is through persistence that we can transform setbacks into triumphs and achieve our dreams.

The Power of Belief:
When Success Shatters Doubt

Introduction:

Success is a profoundly rewarding and exhilarating experience, but its impact is magnified when it is achieved despite the lack of belief or support from others. The journey of overcoming skepticism and doubt becomes an integral part of the narrative, making the taste of success even sweeter. This page explores the remarkable phenomenon of achieving success in the face of disbelief, highlighting the resilience, determination, and self-belief required to turn skeptics into witnesses of one's triumph.

Resilience in the Face of Doubt:

When no one believes in you, it is easy to succumb to self-doubt and question your abilities. However, true champions rise above the negativity and embrace resilience. The absence of external validation can become a powerful driving force, propelling individuals to prove their worth and achieve greatness. The challenges and obstacles faced along the way become stepping stones, allowing individuals to grow stronger and more determined.

Fueling Self-Belief:

In the absence of external support, one's self-belief becomes a crucial source of motivation. It is the unwavering faith in one's capabilities and vision that provides the strength to persevere. Believing in oneself, even when no one else does, is a testament to the power of the human spirit. This self-assuredness instills a sense of purpose and fuels the drive to prove the naysayers wrong.

Pushing Boundaries and Defying Expectations:

When nobody believes in your potential, the opportunity arises to push boundaries and defy expectations. The absence of external expectations allows individuals to set their own standards and redefine what is possible. Unburdened by the limitations imposed by others, they dare to dream bigger, work harder, and innovate beyond what was thought achievable. By exceeding these expectations, they not only surprise those who doubted them but also inspire others to challenge their own perceived limitations.

Building a Strong Support System:

Although success may be sweeter when achieved against all odds, it is essential to acknowledge the importance of a support system. Even if no one initially believed in you, it is crucial to surround yourself with individuals who uplift and encourage your aspirations. As you progress on your journey, you will find like-minded individuals who share your vision and believe in your potential. These individuals become your allies, providing the necessary support and motivation to overcome obstacles.

Impacting Others:

The impact of achieving success against all odds extends far beyond personal triumph. It becomes a testament to the power of determination and serves as an inspiration to those facing their own doubters. By defying expectations, individuals become beacons of hope, reminding others that anything is possible with unwavering belief and relentless effort. Their success not only vindicates their own journey but also paves the way for others to follow their dreams.

Conclusion:

The journey of achieving success when no one believed in you is a testament to the human spirit's resilience and determination. It highlights the power of self-belief, pushing boundaries, and the importance of building a supportive network. The triumph over skepticism not only brings personal fulfillment but also inspires others to pursue their own ambitions. So, let success hit different when no one believed in you, for it is through overcoming doubt that true greatness is achieved.

Setting Aside Pride:
The Pathway to Success

∙∙∙∙∙∙∙●∙●∙●∙●∙●∙●∙●∙∙●∙∙●∙∙∙∙∙

Introduction:

I n the pursuit of our goals and aspirations, there are times when we must set aside our pride and ego to navigate the path towards achievement. The adage "sometimes we have to put our pride to the side to get to where we need to be" encapsulates the essence of humility and resilience required to overcome obstacles and reach our desired destinations. This page delves into the significance of setting aside pride, exploring the benefits, challenges, and transformative power it holds in our personal and professional lives.

The Power of Humility:

Pride, while often associated with confidence and self-assuredness, can sometimes hinder our progress. It blinds us to our weaknesses, prevents us from acknowledging our mistakes, and inhibits personal growth.

Humility, on the other hand, opens doors to self-reflection, learning, and the ability to adapt. By acknowledging our limitations and embracing humility, we gain the capacity to explore new perspectives, seek guidance from others, and make necessary adjustments to our course.

Overcoming Ego for Collaboration:

Setting aside pride becomes particularly crucial when collaboration is involved. In team settings, the ability to work harmoniously and effectively with others is essential for success. Ego-driven behaviors such as stubbornness, a refusal to listen, or an unwillingness to compromise can lead to conflicts and hinder progress. By humbling ourselves and valuing the contributions of others, we foster an environment of mutual respect, cooperation, and innovation. This willingness to put our pride aside enables us to build stronger relationships, achieve shared goals, and maximize our potential.

Learning from Failure:

Failure is an inevitable part of life's journey, and it often presents a critical choice between allowing pride to consume us or using it as a catalyst for growth. When faced with setbacks or mistakes, our pride can tempt us to deny responsibility, blame external factors, or avoid acknowledging our flaws. However, by embracing humility and setting pride aside, we gain the capacity to accept failure as a valuable learning experience. It enables us to take ownership of our actions, identify areas for improvement, and develop resilience to bounce back stronger.

Embracing New Perspectives:

Pride can sometimes limit our willingness to explore alternative viewpoints and ideas. When we put our pride aside, we become open to diverse perspectives, experiences, and knowledge that can enrich our understanding and broaden our horizons. By actively seeking out different opinions, we can challenge our preconceived notions, refine our thinking, and arrive at more innovative and well-rounded solutions. This ability to set aside pride enables personal and intellectual growth, enabling us to adapt to changing circumstances and stay ahead in an ever-evolving world.

Conclusion:

In the pursuit of our goals, it is essential to recognize that sometimes we must put our pride aside to reach our desired destinations. By embracing humility, we unlock the power to learn from our mistakes, collaborate effectively, and adapt to new circumstances. While pride has its place, knowing when and how to set it aside enables personal and professional growth, fostering resilience, openness, and a greater capacity for success. Let us remember that true strength lies not in ego, but in the willingness to be humble and constantly evolve on our path towards fulfillment.

The Consequences of Revenge:
Reflecting on Our Actions

Introduction:

In our community, it is common to hear phrases like "hit back" and "get revenge" when someone wrongs us. These ideas are deeply ingrained in our upbringing, emphasizing the importance of retaliating against those who have harmed us. However, it is crucial to consider what happens after we seek revenge. Revenge is not without consequences; it often invites a cycle of negative outcomes and karma that can surpass the harm we initially endured. This passage urges us to pause and reflect on the repercussions of our actions, encouraging a more thoughtful approach to resolving conflicts. Additionally, it suggests that relying on a higher power to address injustice can help us maintain our moral integrity.

The Vicious Cycle of Revenge:

When we seek revenge, we tend to perpetuate a cycle of negativity. While retaliating might provide momentary satisfaction, it can lead to prolonged animosity, escalating the conflict beyond its original scope. By "hitting back" without considering the consequences, we risk amplifying the harm inflicted upon us, trapping ourselves in a never-ending loop of retaliation. This cycle of revenge can strain relationships, breed resentment, and generate further conflict, ultimately causing more damage than the initial wrong.

Karma: The Law of Cause and Effect:

The concept of karma suggests that our actions have consequences, both in this life and beyond. When we engage in vengeful acts, we generate negative karma, which can manifest in various ways. By seeking revenge, we not only harm others but also harm ourselves spiritually and emotionally. The negative energy we put out into the world can rebound back to us, leading to unforeseen and potentially devastating repercussions. Understanding the karmic effects of revenge can serve as a deterrent, compelling us to consider alternative paths for resolution.

The Importance of Thinking Before Acting:

One of the core messages in this passage is the significance of pausing to reflect before acting out of revenge. Often, in the heat of the moment, our judgment becomes clouded, and we act impulsively, failing to consider the long-term consequences of our actions. By taking a step back, we can assess the situation objectively and make informed choices. Most battles are not worth fighting, and sometimes the best course of action is to let go, forgive, and move forward with our lives. By practicing restraint and thoughtfulness, we can break the cycle of revenge and foster a more peaceful existence.

Divine Intervention and Letting Go:

The passage concludes by suggesting an alternative perspective. Instead of taking matters into our own hands, it proposes allowing a higher power, symbolized as God, to handle our "dirty work." By surrendering our desire for revenge and trusting in a higher justice, we can keep the burden of karma solely on the other person. This approach emphasizes the importance of forgiveness and maintaining our own moral integrity, even in the face of injustice. It encourages us to find solace in the belief that, ultimately, fairness and balance will be restored.

Conclusion:

The passage sheds light on the often-neglected consequences of seeking revenge. It invites us to rethink our conditioned responses and consider the bigger picture. Revenge, although tempting, perpetuates negative cycles, generates karmic repercussions, and can lead to greater harm than the initial wrongdoing. By pausing to reflect, thinking before acting, and embracing forgiveness, we can break the cycle of revenge, promote harmony, and trust that justice will prevail.

Embracing Our Imperfections:
The Power of Therapy and Self-Reflection

Introduction:

I n a world filled with complexities and challenges, it is undeniable that we all have issues. However, what sets us apart is our ability to accept this truth without taking offense. Acknowledging our struggles and recognizing the toxic traits that may have developed within us is the first step towards personal growth. It is essential to understand that the way we perceive our lives as "normal" is often influenced by our upbringing. In this passage, we are reminded of the significance of therapy and the valuable insights it can provide. This essay explores the idea of self-reflection, the benefits of seeking therapy, and the importance of embracing the healing journey.

Accepting Our Imperfections:

The passage reminds us that we all have our own walks of life, and these experiences can shape us in ways that we may not even realize. Sometimes, it is difficult to acknowledge our flaws or toxic traits because they have become deeply ingrained in our behavior patterns. We may dismiss feedback from loved ones, rationalizing that they also have their own issues. However, this attitude can hinder our personal growth. By accepting that we all have imperfections, we create an opportunity for self-improvement and healing.

The Power of Therapy:

Therapy offers a unique space for self-discovery, growth, and healing. It provides a safe and non-judgmental environment where individuals can explore their thoughts, emotions, and behaviors. Unlike friends or family members who may be biased or emotionally invested, a therapist offers an objective perspective. They can help us identify blind spots, uncover the root causes of our issues, and provide guidance on how to navigate through them. Therapy allows us to gain a deeper understanding of ourselves, promote self-awareness, and develop healthier coping mechanisms.

Embracing Insights from Strangers:

Interestingly, the passage highlights that we may sometimes be more receptive to feedback from strangers than from those close to us. This reaction stems from a belief that strangers are not influenced by personal biases or vested interests. While it is true that unbiased feedback can be valuable, it is also essential to remember that the people who care about us deeply often have our best interests at heart. The key lies in being open to feedback from various sources and evaluating them objectively. This openness can lead to personal growth and transformation.

The Need for Healing:

The passage concludes with a call to open ourselves to the idea of therapy if we haven't already done so. It recognizes that many of us can benefit from a little healing. Just as physical wounds require care and attention, emotional wounds also demand healing. Engaging in therapy can empower us to address underlying issues, resolve past traumas, and develop resilience. It is an investment in our well-being and personal growth.

Conclusion:

Accepting our imperfections and acknowledging the influence of our experiences is crucial for personal growth. Therapy provides a valuable resource to navigate the complexities of life, offering professional guidance, self-reflection, and healing. By being open to insights from both familiar and unfamiliar sources, we can gain a broader perspective on ourselves and our behaviors. Remember, we all have issues, but it is through accepting and working on them that we can strive for a healthier and more fulfilling life. Embrace the idea of therapy and embark on a journey of self-discovery, growth, and healing.

Transforming Dreams into Reality:
The Path to Success

·········•••••••••••••••········

Introduction:

In life, it is often said that dreams are the fuel that ignites our passions and drives us towards achieving our goals. However, dreams alone are not enough to turn aspirations into tangible achievements. The passage emphasizes the importance of action and dispels the notion that success can be attained through mere daydreaming. This page explores the significance of perseverance, hard work, and determination in transforming dreams into reality.

Embracing the Reality of Success:

Dreams provide us with a vision of what we desire, but it is essential to acknowledge that the path to success is not paved with shortcuts. Many individuals fall into the trap of wishful thinking, hoping that their dreams will manifest effortlessly. However, the truth is that success requires more than idle fantasies. It demands commitment, effort, and a willingness to face challenges head-on.

The Power of Action:

Dreamers often find solace in their visions, experiencing moments of respite and contentment within the realm of their imagination. However, dreams alone will not bring about significant change or accomplishments. It is only through action that dreams can be transformed into reality. Taking the first step, however small it may be, is crucial in initiating the journey towards success.

Perseverance and Hard Work:

While dreams may be the spark, perseverance and hard work are the driving forces behind transforming them into reality. Success rarely comes overnight; it is the result of relentless effort, determination, and an unwavering belief in oneself. It requires consistent dedication to personal growth, overcoming obstacles, and learning from failures along the way. Every setback is an opportunity to learn and refine one's approach.

Facing Challenges and Adversity:

The pursuit of turning dreams into reality is not without its fair share of challenges and adversity. Roadblocks and obstacles are inevitable on the path to success. However, it is in these moments that true character is tested and resilience is forged. Embracing challenges as opportunities for growth and learning allows dreamers to develop the necessary skills to overcome hurdles and propel themselves forward.

Continuous Growth and Learning:

Success is not a destination but rather a journey of continuous growth and learning. Dreamers must be willing to acquire new knowledge, hone their skills, and adapt to changing circumstances. By embracing a growth mindset, individuals can expand their capabilities and seize opportunities that align with their dreams.

Conclusion:

The passage emphasizes that rest alone is not enough for dreamers; action is required to transform dreams into reality. Success is a result of perseverance, hard work, and a steadfast commitment to personal growth. By embracing challenges and continuously learning, individuals can navigate the path towards success with resilience and determination. Remember, there are no shortcuts; it is through consistent effort and an unwavering belief in oneself that dreams can be turned into reality.

NEGRO(W) | AL MADDIN

Generational Wealth Starts with One Risk Taker

G enerational wealth is a concept that refers to the accumulation of assets and financial resources passed down from one generation to the next. It is often seen as a way to provide a solid foundation for future family members, enabling them to enjoy a higher standard of living and more opportunities. While generational wealth may seem like a lofty goal, it all begins with one individual who is willing to take risks and pave the way for future prosperity.

The passage emphasizes the importance of being that one person—the risk taker, the visionary, the faith walker, the doer—who can make a significant difference in their family's financial trajectory. This person takes the initiative to break free from the status quo and proactively shapes their own destiny. By doing so, they lay the groundwork for creating generational wealth.

One of the first steps mentioned in the passage is to fix your credit. Credit plays a crucial role in financial stability and wealth creation.

By improving one's creditworthiness, individuals gain access to favorable loan terms, lower interest rates, and increased borrowing power. This, in turn, enables them to make strategic financial decisions and leverage opportunities that can have a lasting impact on their family's financial future.

Starting a business is another key element highlighted in the passage. Entrepreneurship offers tremendous potential for wealth creation. By starting a business, individuals can generate income, build assets, and create employment opportunities not only for themselves but also for others. Successful entrepreneurship can lead to the creation of a legacy business that can be passed down through generations, contributing to the long-term growth of generational wealth.

Making investments is also emphasized as a crucial step in the pursuit of generational wealth. Investments provide the opportunity for financial growth and the potential for passive income streams. By wisely investing their resources, individuals can generate wealth that can be passed down to future generations. Investing requires a willingness to take calculated risks, research potential opportunities, and diversify one's portfolio to mitigate potential losses.

The passage encourages individuals to embrace risk and not be afraid of it. Risk-taking is an essential component of wealth creation. Without taking risks, there is limited potential for significant financial growth. Stepping outside of one's comfort zone and embracing uncertainty can lead to opportunities that would otherwise remain inaccessible. By being the one who dares to take risks, individuals set themselves apart from the crowd and position themselves for greater success.

Taking risks and pursuing generational wealth is not without challenges. It requires resilience, determination, and perseverance in the face of setbacks and failures. However, the potential rewards are substantial. By being the catalyst for change within their family, individuals have the power to transform their family's financial trajectory for generations to come.

In conclusion, generational wealth starts with one risk taker—a person who possesses vision, faith, and the drive to take action. By fixing their credit, starting a business, making investments, and embracing risk, this individual becomes the catalyst for change within their family. Their actions create a ripple effect that can lead to significant shifts in their family's financial circumstances. So, be that person for your family and watch how things shift as you pave the way for generational wealth.

Securing the Future:
Passing Down Wealth to Future Generations

········ • • • • • ● • • • • • ·····

Introduction:

The passage "Your children should inherit land, invest-ments, insurance, and businesses not shoes and clothes" encapsulates an important aspect of financial planning and intergenerational wealth transfer. In this modern era, where mate-rial possessions often take precedence, it is crucial to emphasize the long-term benefits of leaving behind assets that can provide financial security and foster growth for future generations. This page delves into the significance of inheriting land, investments, insurance, and businesses, highlighting the advantages they offer over more transient possessions like shoes and clothes.

Wealth Preservation and Accumulation:

Inheriting land, investments, insurance policies, and businesses ensures that children receive assets with the potential to appreciate and grow over time. Unlike shoes and clothes, which are subject to wear and tear and typically lose value, these inheritances represent durable assets capable of preserving and accumulating wealth. Land, for instance, can appreciate in value over the years, making it an excellent long-term investment. Investments, such as stocks, bonds, or real estate, offer the potential for capital appreciation and ongoing income generation. Furthermore, insurance policies can provide financial protection against unforeseen events, mitigating risks and safeguarding the family's financial stability. Lastly, inheriting a well-established business not only offers ongoing income but also allows for the continuation of entrepreneurial endeavors and the potential for further growth.

Financial Security and Independence:

Passing down durable assets empowers future generations to build a strong financial foundation. Inheriting land can provide a stable source of income through rent or agricultural activities, offering financial security and reducing reliance on external factors. Investments generate dividends, interest, or capital gains, enabling individuals to meet their financial needs and pursue personal goals. Insurance policies act as a safety net during challenging times, protecting against unexpected expenses or loss of income. Moreover, inheriting a business can create opportunities for self-employment, entrepreneurship, and wealth creation. These inheritances not only enhance financial security but also foster a sense of independence, allowing individuals to explore their passions and contribute positively to society.

Wealth Transfer and Generational Advancement:

By passing down land, investments, insurance policies, and businesses, parents can empower their children to continue the family's legacy and drive intergenerational advancement. These inheritances provide a platform for future generations to leverage their acquired assets, generate wealth, and make informed financial decisions. In contrast, inheriting shoes and clothes may offer temporary satisfaction, but they lack the transformative power to secure a prosperous future. By prioritizing durable assets, parents instill the values of responsibility, long-term planning, and financial literacy, equipping their children with the tools necessary to navigate the complexities of wealth management and create a lasting impact.

Conclusion:

Inheriting land, investments, insurance policies, and businesses represents a strategic and forward-thinking approach to securing the financial well-being of future generations. By prioritizing durable assets over transient possessions, parents ensure that their children have the means to thrive and prosper. Land and investments offer the potential for appreciation and ongoing income, insurance policies provide financial protection, and inheriting a business fosters entrepreneurship and wealth creation. These inheritances not only provide financial security but also empower individuals to forge their own path, contribute to society, and perpetuate a legacy of success. In essence, by focusing on durable assets, we set the stage for a brighter future, one where our children can confidently navigate the complexities of wealth and achieve their aspirations.

Nurturing Dreams:
Empowering Children for Success

·····•••••••••• ● ••••••••·····

Introduction:

The passage above emphasizes the importance of supporting and encouraging children's dreams and ambitions. It calls attention to the detrimental effects of parental insecurities and the significance of instilling confidence and a can-do attitude in young minds. This page explores the reasons why parents should empower their children to pursue their dreams and provides guidance on how to foster an environment that nurtures their aspirations.

1. Recognizing the Potential:

Children possess a remarkable imagination and untapped potential. Their dreams may appear unconventional or ambitious, but it is crucial to remember that many groundbreaking ideas and successful ventures emerged from such innovative thinking. By supporting their dreams, parents can help unlock their children's hidden talents and abilities.

2. Encouraging Self-Belief:

Parents often play a significant role in shaping their children's self-confidence. When parents exhibit self-doubt or project their own insecurities onto their children, it can hinder their confidence and ability to take risks. Encouraging self-belief allows children to embrace their dreams with enthusiasm, resilience, and determination.

3. Fostering a Growth Mindset:

A growth mindset promotes the idea that intelligence and abilities can be developed through effort, practice, and perseverance. By cultivating a growth mindset in children, parents empower them to view challenges as opportunities for growth. This mindset enables children to overcome obstacles and persist in the pursuit of their dreams.

4. Nurturing Passion and Curiosity:

Children's dreams often stem from their passions and interests. Encouraging and supporting these interests allows them to explore their potential and discover their true passions. Parents should provide resources, opportunities, and mentorship to foster their children's curiosity, helping them develop a deep love for learning and innovation.

5. Embracing Failure as a Learning Opportunity:

Failure is an inevitable part of any journey towards success. Parents should teach children that setbacks and failures are valuable learning experiences, not reasons to give up. By instilling resilience and a positive attitude towards failure, parents equip their children with the courage to pursue their dreams despite obstacles.

6. Balancing Realism with Possibility:

While it is important to support children's dreams, parents also play a role in helping them evaluate the feasibility of their ideas. Offering guidance and constructive feedback can help children understand the practical aspects of their dreams without dampening their enthusiasm. Balancing realism with possibility encourages critical thinking and adaptability.

7. Providing Resources and Opportunities:

Parents can actively support their children's dreams by providing the necessary resources and creating opportunities for growth. This may include enrolling them in relevant classes or extracurricular activities, connecting them with mentors in their desired field, or fostering a supportive network of like-minded individuals.

Conclusion:

As parents, it is crucial to embrace a mindset that empowers our children to pursue their dreams. By nurturing their confidence, providing guidance, and creating a supportive environment, we can equip them with the tools they need to turn their aspirations into reality. Let us stop killing their dreams and instead pass down the invaluable gifts of confidence, self-belief, and unwavering support. Who knows, the idea they have today might just be the next groundbreaking innovation that shapes the future.

NEGRO(W) | AL MADDIN

The Power of Association:
Guilt and Success

Introduction:

The saying "You can be guilty by association and you can be successful by association" highlights the significant impact our social circles have on our actions and achievements. This passage emphasizes the role of association in determining the paths we choose, suggesting that the company we keep influences our behavior and the outcomes we experience. By examining the influence of association on guilt and success, we can understand the importance of selecting our circle of influence wisely.

Guilt by Association:

Being guilty by association refers to the idea that individuals can be implicated or held responsible for the actions, beliefs, or values of the people they associate with. When surrounded by negativity, it becomes challenging to make positive choices and maintain one's moral compass. Negative influences can erode our principles and tempt us to engage in behaviors that may not align with our personal values. Peer pressure and the desire to fit in can override our better judgment, leading to regrettable decisions.

Negative associations can have severe consequences, both personally and socially. In legal settings, guilt by association can result in individuals being implicated in criminal activities due to their connections with others involved. Moreover, associating with individuals who engage in harmful or unethical behaviors can tarnish one's reputation, credibility, and even limit future opportunities.

Success by Association:

Conversely, being successful by association suggests that the people we surround ourselves with can have a positive influence on our aspirations, mindset, and achievements. When we are in the company of motivated and supportive individuals, their optimism and determination can inspire us to strive for excellence. Positive associations encourage personal growth, foster collaboration, and provide valuable support systems that enable us to overcome obstacles and reach our goals.

Choosing our Circle Wisely:

The passage underscores the importance of consciously selecting our circle of influence. By surrounding ourselves with individuals who exhibit qualities and values we admire, we increase our chances of making constructive choices and pursuing success. A supportive network can provide guidance, encouragement, and accountability, helping us navigate challenges with resilience and determination.

To choose our circle wisely, it is essential to evaluate the values, attitudes, and behaviors of the people we spend time with. It does not mean abandoning existing relationships, but rather being discerning about the influence they have on our lives. Seeking out mentors, joining professional or interest-based communities, and cultivating relationships with individuals who inspire and motivate us can contribute to personal and professional growth.

Conclusion:

Association plays a significant role in shaping our lives, impacting both our guilt and our success. Surrounding ourselves with negative influences can lead us astray, cloud our judgment, and result in feelings of guilt. Conversely, positive associations can propel us towards success, fostering personal development, and providing valuable support. By choosing our circle wisely, we can align ourselves with individuals who uplift, encourage, and help us become the best versions of ourselves.

Building Your Dream:
Prioritizing Personal Growth and Entrepreneurship

Introduction:

In today's fast-paced world, it is easy to get caught up in the pursuit of success and lose sight of our own dreams and aspirations. The passage urges individuals to shift their focus from building someone else's company to building their own dreams. This page explores the importance of dedicating our time and energy to personal growth and entrepreneurship, emphasizing the benefits of pursuing our own ambitions.

1. Embracing Personal Fulfillment:

Dedicating our focus towards building up our dreams allows us to tap into our passions and find personal fulfillment. When we work on something we genuinely care about, our motivation and drive increase exponentially. By redirecting our efforts from serving someone else's vision to nurturing our own, we unlock the potential for greater happiness and satisfaction in our lives.

2. Taking Control of Our Destiny:

Becoming our own boss is a goal many individuals aspire to achieve. It provides us with the freedom to make decisions, set our own priorities, and shape our destiny according to our values and aspirations. Instead of spending our time and energy working tirelessly to fulfill someone else's vision, we have the opportunity to channel that effort into creating something that is uniquely ours.

3. Nurturing Entrepreneurial Spirit:

Building our own dream requires an entrepreneurial mindset. It encourages us to think creatively, take calculated risks, and develop a resilient attitude towards challenges. By focusing on our own entrepreneurial endeavors, we cultivate essential skills such as problem-solving, decision-making, and adaptability, which are invaluable in today's competitive landscape. Embracing entrepreneurship allows us to explore uncharted territories, innovate, and make a lasting impact on our chosen field.

4. Creating Opportunities:

Building our dream also opens up doors for others. By establishing our own venture, we have the power to create employment opportunities, contribute to the economy, and support our local communities. As we grow and succeed, we can inspire and mentor others who aspire to follow their own paths. Building a successful enterprise not only benefits us individually but also has a ripple effect that positively impacts those around us.

5. Overcoming Challenges:

Building one's dream is not without its challenges. It requires dedication, perseverance, and resilience. However, the difference lies in the fact that these challenges are directly tied to our own goals and aspirations. The passion and drive we have for our dreams help us navigate obstacles with determination and tenacity. Every setback becomes an opportunity for growth, and every success becomes a testament to our hard work and commitment.

Conclusion:

In a world where many of us spend the majority of our waking hours working for someone else's vision, it is crucial to remember the importance of building our own dreams. By redirecting our focus, investing our time and energy into personal growth and entrepreneurship, we unlock the potential for personal fulfillment, empowerment, and a sense of purpose. Building our dream not only benefits us but also enables us to create opportunities for others and make a lasting impact on the world around us. So, let us embrace the challenge, take control of our destiny, and embark on the journey of building our own dreams.

Overcoming the Hurdle:
Patience and Persistence in Achieving Results

Introduction:

In the pursuit of success, individuals often encounter numerous challenges and obstacles that can deter them from reaching their goals. One of the most significant hurdles that people face is the tendency to quit before witnessing the desired results. This passage highlights the importance of perseverance and patience by emphasizing that winners are those who understand the process required to achieve results. It acknowledges that success takes time and requires unwavering dedication and discipline, urging individuals not to give up when immediate success eludes them. This page delves into the profound insights embedded within this passage, emphasizing the significance of persistence in the face of adversity and offering encouragement to those on their path to success.

The Power of Perseverance:

Perseverance is a trait shared by successful individuals across various domains. It is the ability to persist and remain steadfast in the face of challenges, setbacks, and delays. Many great achievements throughout history were the result of relentless effort and an unwavering commitment to the pursuit of one's goals. Whether in business, sports, or personal endeavors, those who triumph often do so because they refused to give up, even when faced with immense difficulties.

The Role of Time and Patience:

The passage underscores the fact that time is a crucial factor in achieving significant results. Instant success is a rare occurrence, and it is important to understand that true progress often takes considerable time and effort. Patience is key when working towards long-term goals. It involves maintaining faith in oneself and the process, even when the desired outcomes do not materialize immediately. In today's fast-paced world, where instant gratification is highly sought after, cultivating patience has become an increasingly valuable skill.

The Importance of Discipline:

Discipline serves as the backbone of perseverance and patience. It is the ability to adhere to a set of rules, principles, or routines that drive progress towards a goal. Discipline keeps individuals focused and motivated, helping them maintain momentum during challenging times. By practicing self-discipline, individuals develop the resilience needed to overcome obstacles and setbacks. It enables them to push through difficulties, even when the allure of quitting becomes enticing.

Learning from Winners:

The passage asserts that winners can provide invaluable guidance and inspiration. Successful individuals who have achieved the desired results can offer insights into the strategies, mindset, and actions that led to their accomplishments. By studying and emulating their approaches, individuals can gain a deeper understanding of the process required to succeed. It is crucial to recognize that winners faced their fair share of setbacks and failures, but it was their determination and refusal to quit that ultimately propelled them towards success.

Conclusion:

Quitting before seeing the desired results is a common stumbling block on the path to success. The passage highlights the significance of perseverance, patience, and discipline in overcoming this hurdle. It encourages individuals to view setbacks and delays as opportunities for growth rather than reasons to give up. By understanding that success takes time and effort, individuals can harness their inner strength and continue moving forward. Embracing the wisdom of winners and learning from their experiences provides invaluable insights that can guide individuals towards their own triumphs. Ultimately, those who persist and remain dedicated are the ones who have the best chance of achieving their desired results.

The Power of Words:
Manifesting a Positive Life

····•·•·•·•·•·•·**●**·•·•·•·•·•·•····

Introduction:

The passage "Everything I ever said I would do or get has ALL come to life. Don't underestimate the power of your tongue" emphasizes the immense influence our words have on shaping our reality. It highlights the significance of speaking positively, fostering optimistic thoughts, and surrounding ourselves with positive energy to manifest a more fulfilling and positive life. This page explores the profound impact of our words and thoughts on our experiences and provides insights into how we can harness this power to create the life we desire.

1. The Power of Spoken Words:

Words possess an incredible ability to shape our perception of ourselves, our circumstances, and our future. When we consistently speak positively about our goals, aspirations, and desires, we are effectively setting intentions and sending signals to the universe about what we want to manifest. By vocalizing our dreams and ambitions, we strengthen our focus and commitment, aligning our thoughts and actions towards achieving them. The power of spoken words lies in their ability to establish a positive mindset, bolster self-belief, and attract opportunities that align with our desires.

2. The Influence of Thoughts:

Our thoughts act as the building blocks of our reality. When we consistently harbor positive thoughts, we create a mental environment conducive to growth, happiness, and success. Positive thoughts generate a sense of optimism, resilience, and determination, enabling us to overcome challenges and setbacks with a proactive mindset. Moreover, a positive thought pattern enhances our creativity, problem-solving abilities, and overall well-being. By consciously directing our thoughts towards positivity, we can reshape our perception of the world and attract positive experiences.

3. The Law of Attraction:

The concept of the Law of Attraction suggests that we attract into our lives what we focus on, whether positive or negative. Like attracts like, and therefore, by aligning our thoughts, words, and emotions with positivity, we invite positive outcomes and experiences. Surrounding ourselves with positive energy, such as uplifting people, inspirational books, or motivational resources, strengthens our belief in our abilities and reinforces our optimistic mindset. The Law of Attraction reminds us that we have the power to create our reality through our thoughts and emotions, encouraging us to cultivate positivity in all aspects of our lives.

4. Practical Steps towards a Positive Life:

a. Affirmations: Engage in daily affirmations by consciously speaking positive statements about yourself, your goals, and your aspirations. Repeat affirmations that resonate with you and align with your desired reality, reinforcing your belief in your capabilities.

b. Gratitude Practice: Cultivate a sense of gratitude by acknowledging and appreciating the positive aspects of your life. Gratitude shifts your focus to the abundance around you, attracting more positivity and amplifying feelings of joy and contentment.

c. Mindful Awareness: Develop awareness of your thoughts and language patterns. Replace negative self-talk or limiting beliefs with empowering and positive statements. Challenge any negative thoughts that arise and reframe them into more constructive perspectives.

d. Surroundings: Surround yourself with individuals who radiate positivity and support your growth. Engage in activities that uplift your spirits and expose yourself to inspiring content, such as books, podcasts, or motivational speakers.

e. Visualization and Meditation: Dedicate time each day to visualize your goals and dreams as if they have already manifested. Engage in meditation to calm the mind, increase self-awareness, and connect with your inner positivity.

Conclusion:

The passage serves as a reminder of the profound influence our words, thoughts, and energy have on shaping our lives. By embracing positivity and intentionally directing our thoughts and language towards what we desire, we tap into the power of manifestation. By speaking positive words, cultivating optimistic thoughts, and surrounding ourselves with positive energy, we can create a reality filled with abundance, success, and happiness. Let us harness the power of our tongues and unleash the transformative potential within us, leading to a more positive and fulfilling life.

Message of the Day:
Embrace Life's Challenges and Embrace Growth

············ ● ● ● ● ● ● ● ● ● ● ● ● ● ● ●············

I n the journey of life, it is important to remember the choices we make and the desires we hold. The passage, "Remember that you asked for growth. Don't be surprised when life challenges you," serves as a poignant reminder of the inherent connection between personal development and the obstacles we encounter along the way. It urges us to embrace the challenges that come our way and view them as opportunities for growth and self-improvement.

As human beings, we possess an innate desire for growth and progress. We yearn for personal development, whether it be in our careers, relationships, or self-discovery. It is this longing that propels us forward, encouraging us to step out of our comfort zones and confront the uncertainties that life presents.

However, growth seldom comes without challenges. Life has a way of testing our resilience, pushing us beyond our limits, and presenting obstacles that may seem insurmountable at first glance. It is during these moments of struggle and adversity that we are given the opportunity to grow, both personally and spiritually.

When we actively seek growth, we are essentially inviting change into our lives. We acknowledge that true transformation requires us to break free from our old patterns and confront our fears head-on. It is through this process that we gain valuable insights, acquire new skills, and develop a stronger sense of self.

Yet, despite our conscious desire for growth, it is common to feel surprised or even overwhelmed when faced with life's challenges. We may question why we are being tested or feel discouraged by the obstacles in our path. However, it is important to remember that these challenges are not meant to break us but rather to mold us into stronger, more resilient individuals.

In retrospect, we often realize that the most significant periods of personal growth in our lives were marked by the most difficult challenges. It is during these times that we discover our true potential, as we dig deep within ourselves to find the strength and determination to overcome obstacles. These challenges force us to confront our weaknesses, learn from our mistakes, and develop new strategies for success.

When we adopt a mindset that welcomes challenges as opportunities, we shift our perspective and empower ourselves to navigate life's hurdles with grace and resilience. Instead of being surprised or discouraged, we can embrace these challenges as catalysts for growth and transformation. Each obstacle becomes a stepping stone, guiding us closer to our aspirations and enabling us to reach new heights.

Ultimately, the message of the day serves as a gentle reminder to remain steadfast in our pursuit of personal growth. It encourages us to recognize that the challenges we face are not setbacks but rather essential components of our journey. By embracing these challenges and viewing them as opportunities, we can embark on a path of continuous self-improvement, self-discovery, and fulfillment. So, let us welcome the challenges that come our way, for they hold the key to our growth and the realization of our true potential.

Embracing Challenges:
The Catalysts for Personal Growth

Introduction:

L ife is an ever-changing journey, and we often find ourselves seeking growth, both personally and professionally. We set goals, make plans, and hope for a better future. However, it is crucial to remember that growth rarely comes without challenges. In fact, it is through these trials and tribulations that we have the opportunity to truly evolve and reach our full potential. In this passage, the importance of expecting and embracing life's challenges as catalysts for personal growth will be explored.

The Nature of Challenges:

Challenges are an inherent part of the human experience. They come in various forms, such as unexpected obstacles, failures, setbacks, or even major life transitions. Initially, it may be tempting to view these challenges as roadblocks or burdens that hinder progress. However, it is essential to shift our perspective and recognize them as opportunities for growth. Challenges force us to step out of our comfort zones, test our limits, and discover untapped reserves of strength and resilience within ourselves.

The Connection Between Challenges and Growth:

Growth occurs when we push ourselves beyond familiar boundaries, confronting the unknown and embracing discomfort. Challenges serve as catalysts that push us to reevaluate our beliefs, behaviors, and capabilities. They compel us to develop new skills, acquire knowledge, and cultivate emotional intelligence. Each challenge we face acts as a stepping stone towards personal growth, enabling us to become stronger, wiser, and more adaptable individuals.

Learning and Self-Reflection:

Challenges provide fertile ground for learning and self-reflection. When we encounter difficulties, we are forced to assess our strategies, identify areas for improvement, and develop resilience. Through self-reflection, we gain valuable insights into our strengths and weaknesses, allowing us to refine our approach and grow from our experiences. The lessons learned from overcoming challenges become valuable assets that empower us to face future obstacles with confidence and tenacity.

Building Resilience:

Resilience is a key attribute developed through facing and overcoming challenges. It is the ability to bounce back from adversity, adapt to change, and persevere in the face of obstacles. By embracing challenges, we strengthen our resilience muscles, enabling us to weather storms and emerge stronger on the other side. Resilience is a vital quality that not only enhances personal growth but also equips us with the tools to navigate the complexities of life with grace and fortitude.

Expanding Comfort Zones:

Challenges have the power to expand our comfort zones, allowing us to break free from self-imposed limitations. When we willingly face adversity, we discover hidden strengths and talents that were previously dormant. Each challenge conquered builds our confidence and encourages us to tackle more significant and complex obstacles. Over time, what was once perceived as challenging becomes familiar territory, and we continue to evolve and grow.

Conclusion:

In the pursuit of growth, it is imperative to acknowledge that challenges are not hindrances but rather transformative opportunities. By reframing our perspective and embracing life's challenges, we open ourselves up to personal growth and development. Challenges prompt us to learn, reflect, and build resilience, ultimately expanding our comfort zones and enabling us to reach our full potential. Remember, when life challenges you, welcome it as a sign of growth and embark on the path of self-improvement with courage and determination.

Taking Responsibility for Personal Growth and Transformation

Introduction:

The passage highlights the significance of taking responsibility for various aspects of our lives, such as poor eating habits, financial habits, and unhealthy relationships, which are often learned or witnessed before the age of 10. While acknowledging that these patterns may have been ingrained in us unintentionally, the passage emphasizes the importance of recognizing our responsibility in changing them. By taking ownership and control of our lives, we can embark on a journey of personal growth and transformation. This page explores the power of personal responsibility and provides insights into how individuals can actively address and improve different areas of their lives.

1. Acknowledging the Influence of Early Programming:

Children are highly impressionable and absorb information from their surroundings. The passage prompts us to reflect on the habits and behaviors we learned or witnessed during our formative years. It recognizes that these early influences might have contributed to the development of detrimental habits or patterns in adulthood. By acknowledging this connection, we can gain insight into the origins of our behaviors and take steps to modify them.

2. Shifting from Blame to Responsibility:

Although the passage acknowledges that the initial programming may not have been our fault, it emphasizes the need to shift from blaming external factors to accepting personal responsibility. Blaming others or circumstances for our current state only perpetuates a victim mentality, limiting our ability to make positive changes. Taking ownership of our choices and actions empowers us to break free from negative patterns and actively work towards personal transformation.

3. The Power of Ownership:

Taking ownership means recognizing that we have the ability to change our circumstances. It involves acknowledging that our choices and behaviors are within our control and that we can make conscious decisions to improve our lives. By embracing ownership, we become active participants in our personal growth and development.

4. Taking Control of Life:

To initiate positive change, it is crucial to take control of our lives. This requires a proactive approach in identifying areas that need improvement and taking decisive action. For instance, in the case of poor eating habits, we can educate ourselves about nutrition, plan and prepare healthy meals, and seek support from professionals if needed. By actively engaging in self-reflection, setting goals, and implementing effective strategies, we regain control over our lives and reshape our habits for the better.

5. Embracing Personal Growth and Transformation:

Taking responsibility and control of our lives opens the door to personal growth and transformation. It enables us to break free from self-limiting beliefs and unhealthy behaviors, fostering positive changes in various aspects of life. Through consistent effort, determination, and a willingness to adapt, we can establish healthier eating habits, improve our financial literacy, cultivate fulfilling relationships, and enhance overall well-being.

Conclusion:

The passage encourages individuals to reflect on their past influences and take responsibility for their lives. By accepting ownership and actively working to change negative patterns, we can embark on a transformative journey of personal growth. While the initial programming may not have been our fault, it is within our power to break free from detrimental habits and create positive change. By taking control of our lives, we can shape a healthier, more fulfilling future for ourselves.

Embracing Personal Growth:
The Importance of Independence

∙∙∙∙∙∙∙●∙∙●∙∙●∙∙●∙∙●∙∙●∙∙∙∙∙

Introduction:

The passage, "If your friends don't want to travel, go without them. If your friends don't want to start a new hobby, do it without them. If your friends don't want to go on a hike, go without them. Don't rob yourself of experiences because your friends aren't ready to grow," encapsulates an essential life lesson about the significance of personal growth and the willingness to embark on new adventures even when our friends may not share the same enthusiasm. This passage encourages individuals to step out of their comfort zones and embrace independence to fulfill their desires and pursue experiences that foster self-development. In this essay, we will explore the reasons why it is crucial to break free from the fear of missing out on life's opportunities due to the reservations of others.

1. Individual Growth and Self-Discovery:

Venturing into new territories, whether it be traveling, exploring hobbies, or engaging in outdoor activities, presents ample opportunities for personal growth and self-discovery. By allowing ourselves to partake in experiences that may lie beyond the comfort zone of our friends, we open the door to learning more about ourselves, our interests, and our capabilities. Engaging in activities independently enables us to develop a stronger sense of self and build resilience, leading to personal growth and a broader perspective on life.

2. Embracing Autonomy and Decision-Making:

Choosing to go on adventures or pursue hobbies without the company of friends allows us to exercise autonomy and decision-making skills. When we rely solely on the consensus of others, we may inadvertently limit our experiences and miss out on valuable opportunities for personal fulfillment. By stepping outside the boundaries of group approval, we take charge of our lives and become active architects of our own happiness.

3. Building Confidence and Self-Reliance:

Embarking on solo endeavors, be it traveling to new destinations or engaging in hobbies, helps foster confidence and self-reliance. When we challenge ourselves to navigate unfamiliar territories independently, we are forced to rely on our own abilities and problem-solving skills. The confidence gained from successfully handling these situations transcends into other aspects of life, empowering us to tackle challenges head-on and overcome obstacles with resilience.

4. Expanding Social Horizons:

Choosing to pursue experiences without the presence of friends can open doors to meeting new people and expanding our social horizons. When we step outside of our immediate social circle, we are more likely to interact with individuals from diverse backgrounds and cultures, fostering personal growth and broadening our perspective on the world. By engaging with new people, we can gain fresh insights, form meaningful connections, and develop a network of friends who share our passions and aspirations.

5. Avoiding Regret and Living Authentically:

Regret often stems from missed opportunities and unfulfilled dreams. When we allow the reservations or hesitations of others to dictate our choices, we risk living a life that is not authentic to our desires and aspirations. Going after what we truly want, even if it means going without our friends, ensures that we live in alignment with our values and passions, leading to a more fulfilling and meaningful existence.

Conclusion:

The passage highlights the importance of embracing personal growth and experiencing life's adventures, regardless of whether our friends share the same enthusiasm. By stepping out of our comfort zones, pursuing independent endeavors, and embracing new experiences, we open ourselves up to a world of opportunities for self-discovery, confidence-building, and personal fulfillment. Ultimately, by not robbing ourselves of these valuable experiences, we can lead lives that are authentic, enriched, and aligned with our true desires. So, if your friends don't want to join you on your journey, remember that it's perfectly okay to go without them and embrace the incredible possibilities that await you.

Embracing Change:
Divorcing Your Old Life for a New and Better Future

························· ● ● ● ● ● ● ● ● ● ● ● ● ● ● ●·····················

Introduction:

I n the pursuit of happiness and fulfillment, many individuals find themselves stuck in a cycle of discontentment, unable to live the life they truly desire. The passage suggests that the reason behind this predicament lies in people's reluctance to let go of their old life. Whether it is due to fear, bad habits, draining relationships, wasted time, or unsupportive friendships, individuals often resist change, hindering their progress towards a new and improved existence. This page delves into the importance of divorcing one's old life, shedding light on the potential rewards and outlining steps to embark on a transformative journey.

NEGRO(W) | AL MADDIN

Breaking Free from Fear:

Fear is one of the most significant obstacles that prevents people from pursuing their dreams. The fear of the unknown, failure, or judgment often keeps individuals confined within the boundaries of their comfort zone. However, true growth and personal development require embracing uncertainty and taking calculated risks. By divorcing their old life, individuals can liberate themselves from the grip of fear, allowing them to explore new opportunities and forge a path towards a more fulfilling future.

Overcoming Bad Habits:

Another aspect that hinders personal growth is the presence of ingrained bad habits. These habits, whether they involve procrastination, self-doubt, or self-sabotage, keep individuals trapped in unproductive cycles. Divorcing one's old life entails breaking free from these negative patterns and replacing them with positive, empowering behaviors. Through self-reflection, awareness, and consistent effort, individuals can gradually let go of detrimental habits and cultivate healthier routines that align with their aspirations.

Reassessing Draining Relationships:

The quality of our relationships plays a significant role in shaping our overall well-being. In many cases, individuals find themselves surrounded by draining relationships that deplete their energy and hinder their personal growth. Divorcing the old life necessitates reevaluating these relationships and making conscious choices about who to keep in one's inner circle. By seeking out supportive and uplifting connections, individuals can create an environment that nurtures their personal and professional aspirations.

Utilizing Time Effectively:

Time is a precious resource, yet it is often squandered on activities that do not contribute to personal growth. Divorcing the old life involves critically examining how time is spent and identifying unproductive habits or distractions. By consciously redirecting their focus towards meaningful pursuits, individuals can make the most of their time and inch closer to the life they desire. This may involve setting clear goals, establishing priorities, and adopting efficient time management strategies.

Cultivating Supportive Friendships:

The people we surround ourselves with significantly impact our mindset and aspirations. Unsupportive friendships can weigh us down, stifling our progress and limiting our potential. Divorcing the old life necessitates seeking out individuals who share similar goals and values, fostering a positive and encouraging support system. By surrounding themselves with like-minded individuals, individuals can receive the motivation, guidance, and support needed to embark on their journey towards a new and better life.

Conclusion:

Living a life that aligns with our dreams and aspirations requires divorcing our old life and embracing change. By confronting and overcoming our fears, breaking free from detrimental habits, reassessing draining relationships, utilizing time effectively, and cultivating supportive friendships, we can create a foundation for personal growth and fulfillment. It is through these transformative steps that individuals can pave the way to a new and improved existence, embracing the life they truly desire. Let go of the old, embrace the new, and embark on a journey of self-discovery and self-actualization.

Understanding Credit:
Empowering Future Generations

·····•·•·•·•·•·●·•·•·•·•·•·•·•·····

Introduction:

In an increasingly interconnected and financially driven world, understanding credit has become a vital life skill. As responsible adults, it is our duty to equip ourselves with the knowledge necessary to make informed financial decisions. However, it is equally important to ensure that we pass on this wisdom to the next generation, ensuring they avoid the pitfalls of bad credit and harmful habits. By teaching our children about credit, we can empower them to make sound financial choices and build a solid foundation for their future.

The Importance of Credit:

Credit plays a significant role in our lives, influencing our ability to secure loans, obtain housing, and even find employment. It represents our financial reputation and reflects how we manage borrowed money. Teaching our children about credit allows them to recognize its importance and the impact it can have on their lives. By understanding credit, they can learn to make responsible financial decisions, avoiding debt traps and building a positive credit history.

Avoiding Bad Credit:

One of the most valuable lessons we can impart to our children is the importance of avoiding bad credit. We can explain to them that accumulating excessive debt, missing payments, and failing to manage credit responsibly can result in a poor credit score. This can lead to higher interest rates, limited financial opportunities, and difficulty in obtaining loans or credit cards in the future. Encouraging them to be mindful of their spending habits, create budgets, and pay bills on time can lay the foundation for a strong credit profile.

Developing Healthy Financial Habits:

Teaching children about credit goes beyond merely avoiding bad credit. It is an opportunity to instill in them a set of healthy financial habits that will serve them well throughout their lives. By fostering an understanding of budgeting, saving, and responsible borrowing, we can empower them to make informed financial choices. Introducing concepts such as the importance of living within one's means, distinguishing between needs and wants, and saving for future goals can help them develop a lifelong habit of financial prudence.

Practical Lessons in Credit Management:

To effectively educate children about credit, it is essential to provide practical lessons in credit management. This could include explaining the factors that affect credit scores, such as payment history, credit utilization, length of credit history, and types of credit used. Discussing the benefits of maintaining a low credit utilization ratio, avoiding unnecessary credit inquiries, and periodically reviewing credit reports can help them understand how their financial actions impact their creditworthiness.

Leading by Example:

In addition to providing theoretical knowledge, it is crucial to lead by example when it comes to credit management. Children often learn through observation, so demonstrating responsible credit behavior in our own lives can reinforce the lessons we teach. By managing our credit responsibly, making timely payments, and avoiding excessive debt, we can serve as role models and inspire our children to adopt similar practices.

Conclusion:

By taking the initiative to teach our children about credit, we empower them to navigate the financial landscape with confidence and prudence. By instilling an understanding of credit and cultivating healthy financial habits, we equip them with the tools necessary to avoid bad credit and make sound financial decisions. As parents and guardians, we have the power to break the cycle of bad credit and provide a strong foundation for our children's financial well-being. Let us seize this opportunity to educate and inspire the next generation to become financially responsible individuals.

Shifting from a Poor Mindset to a Wealth Mindset:
Unlocking Financial Success

········•••••• ● •••••········

Introduction:

I n today's society, financial success and wealth creation are topics that hold great significance. However, merely accumulating money does not guarantee prosperity. It is the way we handle our finances that ultimately determines our level of wealth. The passage emphasizes the importance of adopting a wealth mindset, which entails investing money instead of spending it frivolously. By understanding and internalizing this concept, individuals can reshape their approach to money management and pave the way for long-term financial security and prosperity.

The Pitfall of a Poor Mindset:

The passage begins by highlighting the characteristics of a poor mindset, where the acquisition of money is immediately followed by thoughtless spending. In this mindset, individuals tend to focus solely on the short-term gratification that money can provide. The cycle of earning and spending perpetuates itself without contributing to lasting financial stability. This mindset often leads to a lack of savings, mounting debt, and limited opportunities for growth and advancement.

The Power of a Wealth Mindset:

Contrasting the poor mindset, the passage introduces the concept of a wealth mindset. It emphasizes that true wealth lies not in the amount of money one possesses but rather in how that money is utilized. The foundation of a wealth mindset is the belief that money can be a tool for generating more wealth and financial security. Instead of mindlessly spending earnings, individuals with a wealth mindset prioritize investing their money wisely.

Investment as a Catalyst for Wealth:

Investing is a pivotal element of the wealth mindset. Rather than seeing money as a means to indulge in immediate pleasures, individuals with a wealth mindset recognize the potential for long-term growth and prosperity. Investments can take various forms, such as stocks, real estate, business ventures, or even personal development and education. The primary goal is to allocate money in a manner that generates returns and expands one's financial resources over time.

The Multiplier Effect of Mindful Financial Decisions:

The passage encapsulates the essence of the wealth mindset in its final statement: "More money doesn't make you rich, what you do with that money does!" By internalizing this notion, individuals can break free from the constraints of a poor mindset and embrace the transformative power of mindful financial decisions. The process begins by understanding the difference between spending and investing and recognizing the long-term benefits of the latter. A wealth mindset requires discipline, patience, and a focus on future goals rather than immediate gratification.

Switching to a Wealth Mindset:

Transitioning from a poor mindset to a wealth mindset is a gradual and ongoing process. It involves reshaping one's beliefs, attitudes, and habits concerning money. Here are a few steps to help facilitate this transition:

1. Education: Invest time in learning about personal finance, investing strategies, and wealth creation. Gain knowledge and seek guidance from reputable sources to make informed financial decisions.

2. Goal Setting: Define clear financial goals and establish a roadmap to achieve them. This will provide direction and motivation to consistently invest and grow your wealth.

3. Budgeting and Saving: Develop a budget that prioritizes saving and investing. Cut unnecessary expenses and allocate a portion of your income towards investments.

4. Diversification: Build a diversified investment portfolio to minimize risks and maximize potential returns. Explore various investment options and seek professional advice if necessary.

5. Patience and Long-term Thinking: Understand that wealth creation is a journey that requires time, patience, and a long-term perspective. Avoid chasing quick gains and stay committed to your investment strategy.

Conclusion:

Shifting from a poor mindset to a wealth mindset is crucial for achieving financial success and security. By understanding the significance of investing over spending, individuals can leverage their financial resources to create lasting wealth. Remember, true riches are not solely determined by the amount of money accumulated, but by the knowledge, discipline, and deliberate actions taken with that money. Embrace the power of a wealth mindset and unlock the doors to financial freedom and abundance.

Taming the Ego:
A Pathway to Success and Fulfillment

Introduction:

In the pursuit of success and fulfillment, it is often said that one's biggest enemy is not external factors or competitors but rather an internal adversary: the ego. The ego, a concept rooted in psychology and philosophy, refers to the part of our consciousness that craves recognition, validation, and dominance. While ego can provide a sense of self-worth and confidence, it can also lead to detrimental consequences in various aspects of our lives. This passage highlights the potential dangers of an unchecked ego and emphasizes the importance of self-awareness and self-control to foster personal growth and achieve lasting success.

Ruining Business and Investments:

Business ventures require rational decision-making, strategic thinking, and adaptability. However, when the ego takes center stage, it can cloud judgment and hinder progress. An inflated ego may prevent entrepreneurs and business leaders from acknowledging their mistakes, seeking guidance, or adapting to changing market conditions. It can lead to an overestimation of one's abilities and a reluctance to listen to constructive criticism. Consequently, decisions may be driven by personal pride rather than objective analysis, potentially resulting in poor business outcomes and missed opportunities for growth.

Similarly, the ego can wreak havoc on investments. When driven by the need for immediate gratification or the desire to showcase superiority, individuals may be prone to impulsive and speculative investment decisions. Overconfidence can lead to excessive risk-taking and a failure to consider the potential downsides. Ultimately, an unchecked ego can jeopardize financial stability and long-term wealth creation.

Ruining Relationships:

Healthy relationships thrive on trust, empathy, and mutual respect. However, the ego's relentless desire for superiority can hinder these crucial elements. When the ego dominates, it becomes challenging to genuinely listen to others, acknowledge their perspectives, and collaborate effectively. Constantly seeking validation and putting oneself above others can lead to strained relationships, conflicts, and a lack of meaningful connections.

Furthermore, an unchecked ego may inhibit personal growth within relationships. Instead of recognizing and learning from one's shortcomings, the ego may resist feedback and deflect blame onto others. This defensive behavior impedes personal development and prevents the establishment of open, honest, and constructive communication.

Ruining Opportunities:

Opportunities for personal and professional growth often arise unexpectedly. However, an unchecked ego can impede our ability to recognize and seize these opportunities. A bloated sense of self-importance can lead to a dismissive attitude towards new ideas, suggestions, or collaborations. The ego may convince us that we are already superior or that our current knowledge and skills are sufficient. As a result, we may miss out on transformative experiences, learning opportunities, and potential breakthroughs that could propel us forward.

Keeping the Ego in Check:

Recognizing the potential pitfalls of an unbridled ego is the first step toward personal growth and success. It is vital to cultivate self-awareness and engage in introspection to understand the motives and triggers behind our ego-driven behavior. By embracing humility, we can acknowledge our limitations and actively seek opportunities for growth. Practicing active listening, accepting constructive feedback, and fostering empathy are essential in taming the ego and building meaningful relationships.

Embracing a growth mindset, which focuses on continuous learning and improvement, can counteract the negative effects of the ego. A growth mindset allows us to view setbacks as learning experiences, encourages collaboration, and promotes resilience in the face of challenges.

Conclusion:

In the battle for success and fulfillment, our biggest adversary often resides within ourselves: the ego. Its potential to disrupt businesses, investments, relationships, and opportunities should not be underestimated. By acknowledging the destructive power of the ego and actively working to keep it in check, we can foster personal growth, build strong relationships, and seize opportunities that lead to lasting success and fulfillment. Remember, it's you versus you, and cultivating self-awareness and humility will be the key to triumph.

Unveiling the Clues to Success:
A Journey of Dedication and Growth

Introduction:

In the pursuit of success, many individuals yearn for a roadmap that guarantees achievement. While there isn't a definitive blueprint to success, there are valuable clues and principles that can guide us towards reaching our goals. However, it's important to recognize that true success requires dedication, hard work, and a mindset focused on growth. In this passage, we will explore the key elements that contribute to success and how they can transform our lives.

Investing Time and Effort:

Success is not handed out freely but rather earned through deliberate effort. Unfortunately, many people desire success without being willing to put in the necessary hours of dedication and hard work. It is akin to expecting a bountiful harvest without sowing the seeds. Just as in any other aspect of life, success demands an investment of time, energy, and commitment. Without these fundamental building blocks, the desired outcomes will remain elusive.

Avoiding Negative Influences:

Similar to how a common cold spreads, negative influences can attach themselves to our lives if we allow them to consume our time and energy. Engaging in drama, negativity, or pessimism can create a toxic environment that hinders personal growth and success. Instead, it is crucial to consciously detach ourselves from such detrimental influences. By focusing on positivity, self-improvement, and surrounding ourselves with like-minded individuals, we create an environment conducive to success.

The Power of Education:

Education is a powerful tool that propels individuals towards success. Devoting time to learn and acquire knowledge about the path we wish to pursue is essential. Just as negativity attracts negativity, investing in education and self-improvement attracts success. By continuously expanding our horizons and developing new skills, we equip ourselves with the tools needed to overcome obstacles and seize opportunities.

Embracing Personal Growth:

Achieving success is not solely about external accomplishments but also about personal growth. Each season of our lives presents an opportunity for self-reflection, introspection, and intentional growth.

By recognizing and letting go of what holds us back, we create space for new possibilities and transformation. It requires a commitment to consistently improve ourselves, both personally and professionally, in order to reach new heights.

The Transformative Journey:

Embarking on the journey towards success necessitates a shift in mindset and daily habits. It is a process of intentional growth, where we consciously align our actions with our aspirations. By investing time and effort, avoiding negativity, pursuing education, and embracing personal growth, we set ourselves on a path that inevitably leads to positive change. The transformation that accompanies the pursuit of success extends beyond mere external achievements; it encompasses an inner shift that empowers us to conquer challenges and manifest our dreams.

Conclusion:

While there may not be a definitive blueprint to success, there are valuable clues and principles that can guide us towards achieving our goals. Success demands dedication, hard work, and a willingness to detach from negative influences. By investing time in self-education and personal growth, we equip ourselves with the necessary tools to overcome obstacles and seize opportunities. As we embark on this transformative journey, we open ourselves up to new possibilities and witness the profound impact success can have on our lives. So, let us dedicate this next season of our lives to pursuing success and watch how our lives change for the better.

"Everybody Can't Go: Navigating Personal Growth and Success"

Introduction:

In the pursuit of personal growth and success, it is essential to recognize that not everyone in our lives can accompany us on our journey. The passage titled "Everybody Can't Go" emphasizes the importance of letting go of individuals who may hinder our progress. While it can be challenging to leave certain people behind, it is crucial to understand that their lack of faith and ambition might not align with our own. This page explores the significance of removing such influences in order to reach our full potential and obtain the blessings that await us.

Letting Go for Personal Growth:

Embarking on a path of personal growth often requires us to assess our surroundings and relationships. While it is natural to develop attachments to the people in our lives, we must be discerning about those who uplift us and those who hold us back. It is essential to surround ourselves with individuals who share our goals, aspirations, and a positive mindset. However, there will inevitably be those whose presence impedes our progress.

Obstacles on the Path to Success:

Success is often compared to a balance beam in the passage. Imagine that each person in our lives represents a weight on one side of the beam. If we allow individuals with limited faith and ambition to occupy our journey, their negativity and lack of drive will act as burdens, weighing down our progress. Just as a heavier load causes one side of the balance beam to remain lower, the presence of unsupportive individuals can hinder our growth and hinder our ability to reach our full potential.

Choosing Our Companions:

To thrive and flourish, we must carefully choose the people we surround ourselves with. It is not an act of selfishness or arrogance to prioritize our personal growth. Rather, it is an act of self-awareness and understanding that we have a limited amount of time and energy available to us. By selecting companions who are aligned with our ambitions and who support our journey, we create an environment that fosters personal development and success.

The Courage to Let Go:

Letting go of people who hinder our progress is not an easy task. It requires courage, self-reflection, and a willingness to prioritize our own well-being. However, it is essential to remember that our growth and success are intrinsically tied to our ability to shed negative influences. While it may be painful to part ways with friends, family members, or acquaintances, we must focus on the long-term benefits of surrounding ourselves with those who uplift and inspire us.

Embracing Personal Potential:

By letting go of individuals who hold us back, we create space for new connections and opportunities. Removing negative influences allows us to rise above limitations and reach our full potential. Our journey becomes lighter, enabling us to pursue our ambitions with greater clarity and determination. Embracing the idea that not everybody can go with us empowers us to take control of our lives and make decisions that align with our personal growth and success.

Conclusion:

In the pursuit of personal growth and success, it is important to recognize that not everyone can accompany us on our journey. We must be selective about the individuals we allow into our lives, choosing those who support and uplift us. Letting go of people who hinder our progress can be difficult but is necessary for our own personal development. By embracing the idea that not everybody can go with us, we create space for new opportunities and increase our chances of reaching our full potential. So, let us have the courage to release those who hold us back and forge ahead towards the blessings that await us.

Rising from Rock Bottom:
Embracing the Path of Resilience

Introduction:

Life is a journey filled with ups and downs, and at times, we find ourselves plummeting to what feels like rock bottom. It is during these moments of adversity that we often experience a profound sense of discouragement. However, it is important to recognize that hitting rock bottom should not be seen as an end, but rather as an indication that the only way to go from there is up. Instead of getting mentally stuck in the challenges of the present, it is crucial to embrace resilience and focus on the potential for growth and transformation that lies ahead.

Navigating Rock Bottom:

Rock bottom is a term commonly used to describe a state of extreme adversity, failure, or personal crisis. It could be the loss of a job, a broken relationship, a financial setback, or any situation that leaves us feeling overwhelmed and defeated. In such moments, it is natural to experience negative emotions, self-doubt, and a loss of hope. However, it is essential to recognize that hitting rock bottom can also serve as a powerful catalyst for change.

The Only Way is Up:

When we hit rock bottom, we reach a critical turning point in our lives. It is at this juncture that we have a unique opportunity to reassess our priorities, values, and aspirations. Rock bottom is an invitation to reflect on our choices, learn from our mistakes, and redefine our path forward. Instead of dwelling on the hardships of the present, we can choose to shift our focus towards the potential for growth, self-improvement, and personal transformation.

Resilience in Action:

Resilience is the ability to bounce back from adversity and find strength in the face of challenges. It involves adopting a mindset that acknowledges setbacks as temporary and seeks opportunities for growth. When confronted with rock bottom, it is crucial to cultivate resilience. This can be done by:

1. Accepting the reality: Acknowledge the current situation and allow yourself to feel the emotions associated with it. Avoid denying or suppressing your feelings, as this will only delay the healing process.

2. Learning from the experience: Reflect on the circumstances that led to rock bottom and identify the lessons that can be

gleaned from them. Embrace the opportunity for self-reflection and personal growth.

3. Setting goals: Define your aspirations and establish clear, realistic goals that align with your values. Break them down into manageable steps to create a sense of progress and momentum.

4. Seeking support: Surround yourself with a supportive network of friends, family, or mentors who can offer guidance, encouragement, and a listening ear. Sharing your struggles with others can alleviate the burden and provide fresh perspectives.

5. Cultivating self-care: Take care of your physical, emotional, and mental well-being. Engage in activities that bring you joy, practice mindfulness or meditation, prioritize healthy habits, and celebrate small victories along the way.

Conclusion:

Hitting rock bottom can be a daunting and disheartening experience, but it is crucial to remember that it does not define our future. Instead, it serves as a turning point and an opportunity for growth. By embracing resilience, accepting the reality, learning from the experience, setting goals, seeking support, and practicing self-care, we can navigate our way out of rock bottom and emerge stronger, wiser, and more determined. The journey from rock bottom to soaring heights is within our reach; all we need is the courage to take that first step.

Embrace Vulnerability:
Breaking Down Walls to Embrace Life's Changes

········●●●● ● ●●●●·····

L ife is a journey filled with ups and downs, and along the way, we all accumulate scars and wounds from our past. These experiences can shape us, leading us to build walls to protect ourselves from potential hurt. However, it's essential to recognize that it's okay to let those walls down, to stop being so closed off, and to embrace vulnerability.

Many of us have learned to act tough, believing that showing vulnerability is a sign of weakness. But in reality, allowing ourselves to be open and authentic takes immense strength and courage. It's a profound act of self-love and growth to break free from the confines of our self-imposed barriers.

When we build walls around our hearts, we may believe that we are shielding ourselves from pain, disappointment, and heartache. However, what we often fail to realize is that these walls also prevent us from fully experiencing joy, love, and genuine connections. By allowing ourselves to be vulnerable, we open the door to meaningful relationships, enriching experiences, and the full spectrum of emotions that make us human.

Carrying the wounds from our upbringing is a natural part of the human experience. The events of our past have undoubtedly left a mark on us, shaping our beliefs and behaviors. However, it's crucial to acknowledge that not everyone we encounter in life is out to hurt us. By keeping our defenses up at all times, we might unintentionally shut out potential connections, love, and happiness.

Our experiences, both positive and negative, are opportunities for growth and learning. Instead of letting our wounds define us, we can choose to rise above them and use our past as a stepping stone to a better future. Embracing vulnerability means being honest with ourselves and others about our struggles, hopes, and fears. It allows us to seek support when needed and share our joys and triumphs with those we care about.

Life is an ever-changing journey, and as we move forward, we must be willing to evolve along with it. Bringing an old mentality into a new environment or phase in life can hinder our personal growth and limit our experiences. Embracing change and adapting to new circumstances is key to unlocking new opportunities and discovering our true potential.

Change can be intimidating, and stepping into the unknown can be unsettling. However, by choosing to embrace vulnerability, we create a space for new possibilities and growth. It's about accepting that life is unpredictable and that the only constant is change itself. When we resist change and cling to old ways of thinking, we deny ourselves the chance to evolve and flourish.

Opening up and embracing vulnerability can be daunting, but it paves the way for genuine connections with others. When we allow ourselves to be authentic, we create space for others to do the same, fostering a deeper sense of understanding and empathy within our relationships. It cultivates an environment where people feel seen, heard, and accepted for who they are, not just for what they show on the surface.

Letting your walls down doesn't mean discarding the lessons you've learned or forgetting the past. It means finding a balance between protecting yourself and being receptive to the beauty that life has to offer. By choosing to embrace vulnerability and openness, you embark on a path of self-discovery and personal growth.

So, let go of the fear of being hurt, and start living with a newfound sense of freedom. Embrace life's changes with an open heart, and you'll find that the world becomes a more compassionate and welcoming place. Remember, it's okay to be vulnerable—it's a beautiful part of what makes us human. Embrace your uniqueness, and let your light shine through the cracks of your vulnerability, for that's where true strength and beauty reside.

The Power of Asking for Help:
Overcoming Ego to Embrace Growth

In a world that often celebrates self-reliance and independence, it can be challenging to admit when we need assistance. Our egos tend to get in the way, whispering to us that asking for help is a sign of weakness or inadequacy. However, the truth is far from that - it's okay to ask for help. In fact, it's a powerful act of courage and self-awareness that can pave the way for personal growth and a brighter future.

At times, our egos can deceive us into believing that we have everything figured out. We adopt the "I got it all figured out" mentality, thinking that asking for help is unnecessary because we believe we have all the answers. But the reality is that none of us truly have everything figured out. Life is an intricate journey filled with twists, turns, and challenges that we cannot navigate alone.

Recognizing that there's always room to learn and grow is a humbling and empowering realization. When we embrace the idea that we don't have all the answers, we open ourselves up to the vast array of knowl-edge and wisdom that surrounds us. Every individual we encounter has unique experiences and insights to offer, and by seeking help, we tap into a vast reservoir of collective knowledge.

Asking for help is not a sign of weakness; it's a sign of strength and vulnerability. It takes courage to admit that we don't have it all together and that we need support. By doing so, we create authentic connec-tions with others and cultivate a supportive network that can lift us up in times of need.

When we allow others to help us, we invite positive change and trans-formation into our lives. Blocking blessings can occur when we let our ego hinder us from seeking assistance. There are people around us who genuinely want to see us succeed and thrive, but they can only lend a helping hand if we're willing to reach out and ask.

Human beings are social creatures, and we are wired to connect with one another. Offering help and receiving help are fundamental aspects of our interdependence. It's through this exchange of support that we can build stronger communities and foster a sense of belonging.

Letting go of the notion that we must have it all figured out allows us to be more compassionate toward ourselves. It's essential to remember that we are all continuously learning and evolving. Instead of feeling ashamed of seeking help, we can celebrate our openness to growth and improvement.

Asking for help doesn't diminish our worth; it enhances it. It's a pow-erful tool for personal development, as it enables us to access resources, gain valuable insights, and expand our perspectives. When we open ourselves to learning from others, we create a positive feedback loop of growth and self-improvement.

In conclusion, let go of the ego-driven resistance to asking for help. Embrace the fact that none of us have all the answers, and that's perfectly okay. There's no shame in seeking support, guidance, or a helping hand. Embracing vulnerability and reaching out for assistance can lead us to new opportunities, deepen our connections with others, and propel us towards a more fulfilling and meaningful life journey. So, don't let your ego stand in the way of your growth and happiness—ask for help and let the blessings flow.

Embrace Accountability for Success

A ccountability is the cornerstone of personal and professional growth, paving the way for success and fulfillment. Yet, it's not uncommon to find oneself struggling with this essential trait. If you find that you lack accountability, it's crucial to address this issue and take the necessary steps to overcome it.

The Consequences of a Lack of Accountability

A lack of accountability can have far-reaching consequences, both in our personal and professional lives. When we fail to take responsibility for our actions and decisions, we deprive ourselves of the opportunity to learn and grow. We miss out on valuable learning lessons that can propel us forward on our journey to success.

In the professional realm, accountability is a key factor in building trust and credibility. Colleagues, superiors, and clients all rely on individuals who can be trusted to deliver on their promises and admit their mistakes when they occur. Without accountability, relationships may suffer, and opportunities for advancement might pass us by.

Embracing Accountability as a Catalyst for Growth

Accepting accountability is not about dwelling on our failures or shortcomings. Instead, it's about acknowledging that mistakes are a natural part of life, and they present invaluable chances for growth. By embracing accountability, we open ourselves up to self-improvement and self-awareness, which are vital components of success.

The Learning Lesson in Accountability

When we avoid taking responsibility for our actions, we miss out on the learning lesson that comes with it. Understanding the root causes of our mistakes allows us to identify patterns, make necessary adjustments, and avoid repeating those errors in the future.

Accountability also fosters resilience. When we own up to our missteps, we develop the strength to bounce back and try again. Failure becomes a stepping stone rather than a roadblock, propelling us toward greater achievements.

Steps to Cultivate Accountability

1. Be Honest with Yourself: Take a moment to reflect on your actions and decisions. Be honest about where you might be avoiding accountability.

2. Accept Imperfection: Understand that everyone makes mistakes, and it's okay to be imperfect. Embrace these moments as opportunities to learn and grow.

3. Set Realistic Goals: Break down your goals into achievable steps. This way, you can hold yourself accountable for meeting those smaller milestones.

4. Seek Support: Surround yourself with individuals who encourage accountability and growth. Lean on mentors or friends who can provide constructive feedback.

5. Learn from Role Models: Observe and learn from individuals who exemplify strong accountability traits. Understand how they approach challenges and setbacks.

In Conclusion

Embracing accountability is an empowering choice that can lead to a profound transformation in your life. By taking ownership of your actions, you are paving the way for personal and professional success. Remember, you have the power to shape your path by learning from your mistakes and using them as stepping stones to a brighter future. Embrace accountability, and unlock the door to endless possibilities.

Unshackling the Past:
Embracing the Power of Change

ife is a journey of growth and transformation, and as we evolve, it's natural for us to change. Each day offers us opportunities to learn, adapt, and become better versions of ourselves. However, in this process of personal evolution, we may encounter resistance from others who want to keep us tethered to our past.

Don't Allow Others to Pull You Back:

As we strive to break free from old habits that no longer serve us, it's crucial not to let external influences dictate our path. Sometimes, well-meaning friends or acquaintances from our past might attempt to reintroduce us to the person we used to be. They might express sentiments like, "You've changed" in a negative context, as if it's a bad thing. But we must remember that change is a sign of growth and self-awareness.

The Power of Transformation:

Change is not only a natural part of life but a beautiful one. It signifies that we are willing to evolve, learn from our experiences, and embrace new possibilities. As we shed old layers, we make space for personal growth and open ourselves up to exciting opportunities.

Breaking Free from Guilt:

In the face of others' attempts to make us feel guilty for changing, it's crucial to stay true to ourselves. We shouldn't apologize for outgrowing certain behaviors or mindsets that once defined us. Growth is a testament to our strength and resilience. Embracing change allows us to live authentically and align with our true selves.

Stay Committed to Your Journey:

As we embark on our path of transformation, it's essential to surround ourselves with a supportive network. Seek out individuals who encourage you to embrace change and who appreciate the person you are becoming. Remember, the people who truly care about your well-being will celebrate your growth, not hold you back.

Moving Forward with Confidence:

Let go of the fear of judgment and embrace the changes you've made. You are not defined by your past; you are defined by who you are today and the choices you make in the present. Trust your intuition and continue to pursue the path that aligns with your values and aspirations.

Conclusion:

Embracing change is a powerful act of self-love and empowerment. Don't allow others to undermine your progress or lead you back into patterns you've outgrown. Be proud of the person you are becoming, and remember that your journey is yours alone to define. Keep moving forward with confidence, and let the winds of change carry you towards a brighter and more fulfilling future.

Breaking Free from the "Keeping Up with the Joneses" Trap:
Prioritize Investing for Success

......•••••• ● •••••••...

In today's hyper-connected world, it's easy to fall into the trap of constantly comparing ourselves to others, especially when it comes to financial success and material possessions. The phrase "Keeping Up with the Joneses" aptly describes this behavior, where we strive to match or surpass the lifestyles of our peers, neighbors, or colleagues. However, in this pursuit of keeping up appearances, we often lose sight of what truly matters and jeopardize our own financial well-being.

The Illusion of Success:

The quest to keep up with others can be intoxicating. We see someone with a bigger house, a fancier car, or the latest gadgets, and we feel the pressure to achieve the same or more. Social media amplifies this phenomenon, presenting carefully curated images of seemingly perfect lives, further fueling our desire to keep up. But what lies beneath this facade is often hidden financial strain and stress.

The Perils of Overindulgence:

Blowing most of our wealth to maintain an illusion of success can have serious consequences. It can lead to excessive spending, debt, and an inability to build wealth for the future. Living beyond our means can trap us in a cycle of perpetual financial struggle, where we are always chasing after the next status symbol, never finding true contentment or financial security.

The Power of Prioritizing Investing:

Instead of falling into the "Keeping Up with the Joneses" trap, we need to shift our focus towards prioritizing investing and building a solid financial foundation. Investing is the key to long-term wealth creation and financial freedom. By directing our resources into investment vehicles such as stocks, real estate, retirement accounts, or starting a business, we empower ourselves to grow our wealth steadily and sustainably.

Investing is not just about preparing for the future; it's also about embracing financial responsibility and freedom in the present. When we prioritize investing, we gain the confidence to make well-informed financial decisions and resist the urge to conform to societal pressures. We can break free from the cycle of comparison and redefine our own path to success.

Embracing Financial Independence:

Shifting our mindset from keeping up with others to securing our financial future gives us the freedom to focus on what truly matters to us. It allows us to set meaningful goals, whether it's traveling, pursuing a passion, supporting loved ones, or contributing to causes we care about. Financial independence grants us the autonomy to live life on our terms, without being burdened by the need to impress or outdo others.

Conclusion:

In a world that constantly encourages us to measure our success against others, it's crucial to remember that true success is not defined by material possessions or social status. It's about creating a life of financial security, contentment, and personal fulfillment. Prioritizing investing over trying to "keep up with the Joneses" is the key to breaking free from the cycle of comparison and unlocking the doors to lasting success and happiness. So, let's start investing in ourselves and our future, and pave the way to a more prosperous and fulfilling life.

Don't Spend Too Early:
Invest in Your Future Growth

I n the journey towards success, it's easy to get caught up in the excitement of achieving a level of prosperity. Many of us have experienced that surge of accomplishment and the temptation to upgrade our lifestyles immediately. While it's natural to reward ourselves for our hard work, it's essential to remember that the true goal is to continue growing and building upon our successes.

The trap lies in spending too early, without fully considering the long-term consequences. Premature spending increases our overhead, leaving us with less capital to invest back into our ventures for further growth. It's crucial to resist the allure of immediate gratification and instead adopt a mindset focused on sustainable progress.

The Art of Wise Investment

The key to avoiding the pitfall of premature spending is to prioritize smart investments in our future. Rather than splurging on extravagant purchases, we should allocate resources into ventures that promise long-term returns. Whether it's expanding our business, upskilling ourselves, or diversifying our investments, each decision should be made with the intent of fostering continuous growth.

Building a Strong Financial Foundation

Delaying excessive spending is not about denying ourselves happiness; it's about building a strong financial foundation that can support our dreams for years to come. By resisting the urge to overspend, we position ourselves to seize bigger opportunities and weather any unexpected challenges that may arise.

Mindful Lifestyle Adjustments**

Being cautious about early spending doesn't mean leading a life of scarcity or deprivation. Instead, it encourages us to make mindful lifestyle adjustments. Prioritize experiences over material possessions, and focus on personal development that enriches your knowledge and skills.

The Power of Delayed Gratification

Delayed gratification is a powerful tool in achieving lasting success. By exercising restraint and practicing patience, we open doors to a brighter and more prosperous future. Each dollar saved or reinvested is a step towards financial freedom and greater control over our destiny.

Be the Master of Your Financial Destiny

Let's not fall victim to the allure of immediate but short-lived pleasures. Instead, let's be the master of our financial destiny by recognizing that the journey of growth is ongoing. Embrace the mindset of an investor, always seeking opportunities to compound our success and create a legacy that lasts beyond the present.

Remember, the path to greatness is paved with careful planning, wise investments, and the resolve to resist impulsive spending. Together, let's nurture our dreams, protect our gains, and forge a future defined by sustainable prosperity and abundance.

THE END

········•••••••• ● ••••••••········

Thank You!

Dear Readers,

I am overwhelmed with gratitude as I sit down to write this closing page. It is an honor and privilege to extend my heartfelt appreciation to each and every one of you who took the time out of your lives to read my book, "Negrow." Your support and presence have meant the world to me.

Writing this book was a profound journey, one that compelled me to examine the depths of my soul and confront the complexities of the human experience. Throughout the process, I often found myself humbled by the power of storytelling and the ability of words to bridge gaps, spark conversations, and cultivate understanding.

I want to express my deepest gratitude to all of you for trusting in my guidance as you embarked on this literary adventure. Your willingness to open your hearts and minds to the narrative I crafted fills me with immense joy. It is your curiosity, empathy, and willingness to listen that give purpose to the stories we tell. Your engagement with "Negrow" validates my belief that literature can serve as a powerful force for positive change.

I firmly believe that this idea was placed in my spirit by a higher power. It was my responsibility to share this story, to shed light on the diverse experiences, struggles, and triumphs of individuals often marginalized by society. Your readership has affirmed my conviction, and for that, I am truly grateful.

To my family and friends who have been my pillars of strength and unwavering support throughout this journey, thank you for your encouragement, patience, and love. Your belief in me has been an invaluable source of inspiration.

I extend my deepest gratitude to my publisher, editors, and the entire team who played a vital role in bringing "Negrow" to life. Your dedication, expertise, and commitment to excellence have made this book a reality. I am forever grateful for your hard work and unwavering belief in this project.

Finally, I would like to thank God for entrusting me with this story and providing the guidance and inspiration needed to see it through. It is by His grace that I have been able to share this work with you all.

As you close the final pages of "Negrow," I hope it has left an indelible mark on your heart and mind. May it spark conversations, challenge preconceptions, and foster a more inclusive and compassionate world.

Thank you once again for embarking on this journey with me. Your support means more to me than words can express.

With deepest appreciation,

Al Maddin